The Warrior's Walk

The Warrior's Walk

Keys to Victory in Spiritual Battle

Tracy Tennant

RIGHT TRACK PUBLISHING

SPRINGFIELD, MO

The Warrior's Walk: Keys to Victory in Spiritual Battle
© 2024 by Tracy Tennant

All Rights Reserved. No part of this publication may be produced or transmitted in any form or by any means, including informational storage and retrieval systems, without permission in writing from the copyright holder, except for brief quotations in reviews. Permission granted for use in small group study.

All Scripture quotations, unless otherwise indicated, are taken from the (NASB®) New American Standard Bible®, Copyright © 1960, 1971, 1977, 1995, 2020 by The Lockman Foundation. Used by permission. All rights reserved. lockman.org.

Scripture quotations, indicated as CJB, are taken from the Complete Jewish Bible by David H. Stern. Copyright © 1998. All rights reserved. Used by permission of Messianic Jewish Publishers, 6120 Day Long Lane, Clarksville, MD 21029. www.messianicjewish.net.

Scripture quotations marked (NLT) are taken from the Holy Bible, New Living Translation, copyright ©1996, 2004, 2015 by Tyndale House Foundation. Used by permission of Tyndale House Publishers, Carol Stream, Illinois 60188. All rights reserved.

Scripture quotations marked as TLV, are taken from the Tree of Life Version. Copyright © 2014, 2016 by the Tree of Life Bible Society. Used by permission of the Tree of Life Bible Society.

Right Track Publishing
First Edition March 2024
Printed in the United States of America
ISBN: 978-1-947037-99-1
Cover design by Tracy Tennant
Interior design and layout by Tracy Tennant
Cover photo by Mystic Art Design

Dedicated to the Remnant:
The righteous who shine forth like the sun
in the Kingdom of our Father.

Contents

Introduction 1

How the Battle Began 9

Our Identity in Messiah 15

Authority of the Believer 23

Armor of God: The Belt of Truth 37

Armor of God: The Breastplate of Righteousness 49

Armor of God: The Shoes of the Gospel of Peace 59

Armor of God: The Helmet of Salvation 73

Armor of God: The Shield of Faith 87

Armor of God: The Sword of the Spirit 97

Armor of God: The Cloak of Zeal 111

Armor of God: The Spear of Prayer 123

The Walk of a Warrior 141

Bibliography 147

Introduction

Our battle isn't just about casting out demons or direct hand-to-hand combat with the powers of darkness. Is that something we must deal with at times? Yes, but most of the time the dark side—in terms of both spiritual entities and their human operatives—comes against humanity in both subtle and overt ways through:

- Deception
- False religion
- Occult practices
- "Charged" items (No, not referring to credit cards)
- Mind-altering drugs or pharmaceuticals
- Environmental toxins
- Genetically modified and artificial foods
- Worldly philosophies
- Fake news and propaganda

As I share some of my background with you, take mental note of entryways and circumstances that the demonic realm uses to keep people from knowing the truth or to oppress and harass them. Use your discernment to identify the red flags.

I grew up in a loving, non-religious home. My mother took me to church for a short period of time, only a few months, and that was the end of my religious training and experience. When I was young, I had a lot of nightmares. Most of my bad dreams occurred around the ages of five and six. They were often about monsters trying to get me, chasing me down hallways that never seemed to end. I was afraid to go to sleep at night, so my mother and aunt took turns lying next to me in bed until I fell asleep. I always had to have a night-light on.

My first supernatural experience happened when I was eight-years-old. I had a favorite stuffed animal that my stepdad won for me at a game in a carnival. I named it Herby (a little snake of all things). How I wished Herby would come to life! I talked to Herby as if he were a real pet and told him I wanted him to be alive. I instructed him to let me know that he was more than just a toy, and I set a date for it to happen.

I couldn't wait until that upcoming Saturday, the day I had picked! I was sitting in my grandmother's rocking chair watching cartoons and Herby was on the hassock a few feet away. Suddenly, of its own accord, Herby flew onto my lap. I was thrilled beyond measure! That was the only instance the object moved on its own by an invisible power.

Around the same time, my aunt brought home a Ouija Board from the toy store and thought it would be a fun parlor game to have on hand when company came. Two things I remember; first off, it worked. The planchette moved under the power of an unseen force. The second thing is that my aunt asked the Ouija it if she would ever marry. The planchette spelled out the answer, "When a cat lays an egg." My aunt is now over 90-years old and never married, so I take that as evidence that cats have as yet to lay eggs!

My mom remarried when I was nine-years-old, and we moved into my stepdad's little one-bedroom house that he and his mother shared before she passed away a few months earlier. Guess who had to sleep in the deceased woman's bedroom, in her bed, and in her sheets? Yep, it was me. I overheard my stepdad tell the story of when his mother passed away. She was visiting his sister's house for a few days. My stepdad woke up out of a sound sleep at 4:00 AM, the moment she died, and a cold wind rushed through the house and slammed his mother's bedroom door shut. There were no windows or outer doors open.

After hearing this ghost story, I was terrified at night, and would beg my parents to let me sleep on the sofa in the room with them, but most of the time they said no. They told me I was "a big girl" and needed to learn to sleep alone. The problem was I wasn't alone; there was something scary there with me at night.

By the time I was 11, we had moved out of that house into a larger one. When my aunt and uncle came over on weekends to play cards and drink with my parents, my cousins and I would play games like Light as a Feather, Bloody Mary, and we even held seances. We had no idea what we were doing; we just copied what we saw in the movies or on the weekly Saturday night horror show *Fright Night*, hosted by "Sinister Seymour." We would try to call up the spirits of famous dead people like Paul Revere and other historical figures, and supernatural things would happen, like thuds and knocking on the outside walls of the house.

When my parents went out for the evening on occasion, leaving me at age 12 to babysit my younger step-siblings, I would feel the presence of something else in the house. It made the hair on my arms stand on end. I would call my aunt across town and beg her to come over because I was afraid.

Intrinsically, I knew there was another world or dimension out there, more than could be seen with our physical eyes, and I started reading books about how to develop ESP (Extra Sensory Perception) and how to foretell the future. I learned about omens and divination from the living room bookshelf of a woman up the street who I babysat for and in books I checked out at the library.

After I turned 13, my best friend invited me to a youth activity at her church—*The Church of Jesus Christ of Latter-day Saints* (aka Mormon or LDS Church). It was amazing. I felt like I was coming home. A warm feeling filled me while I was there, and I "knew" that was where I belonged. I was baptized into Mormonism on my 14th birthday.

My parents became tired of the smog, high taxes, the traffic, and the increasing crime, so later that year we moved from Canoga Park, California to Provo, Utah. Provo was my dream destination because I wanted to be where the population was primarily Mormon. I also intended to marry Donny Osmond, assuming I could attract his attention at church. It ended up that Donny started dating a girl from my high school before having the opportunity to fall in love with me, so things didn't exactly pan out the way I had envisioned.

The Warrior's Walk

When I was 16, I experienced my first direct demonic attack. I was upset because it was the night of Junior Prom and my date canceled on me earlier that day. As I was lying in bed crying in the dark, feeling horrible about missing out on my only chance to attend prom, the room suddenly dropped in temperature and I was gripped by an unseen force. I couldn't move or speak. An invisible power held me captive, immobilizing me and preventing me from screaming. My vocal cords were inoperative, as were all my muscles. It was terrifying.

Struggling with all my might I was finally able to let out a yelp, and my aunt, who was in the next room, heard the noise and opened my bedroom door to ask if I was okay. She exclaimed, "Oh, it's so cold in here!" The power that held me bound lifted and the room immediately returned to normal temperature.

Although I had a brush with the powers of darkness, it didn't stop me from reading thrillers or going with friends to horror movies that came out in the theaters. After watching Stephen King's *The Shining*, my boyfriend and I couldn't hardly sleep for weeks because the images from the movie haunted us at night.

I grew up, got married, and started my own family. As a devout Mormon, I began attending the temple, where we took part in ceremonies and rituals rooted in Freemasonry. We took oaths and made covenants for ourselves and on behalf of the dead (our own ancestors and the ancestors of others). At that time, the 1980s, the oaths taken in the temple included patrons pantomiming their own deaths should they reveal the specifics of what went on inside the edifice. As reported by the Los Angeles Times (May 5, 1990, *Mormons Modify Temple Ritual*)[1], the more gruesome covenants were removed from the ceremony;

> "In pledging to never reveal the ritual, Mormons formerly made three motions — drawing one's hand quickly across the throat, another indicating one's heart would be cut out and the third suggesting disembowelment."

---

1. Dart, John. "Mormons Modify Temple Rites : Ceremony: Woman'S Vow to Obey Husband Is Dropped. Changes Are Called Most Significant since 1978." Los Angeles Times. May 5, 1990. https://www.latimes.com/archives/la-xpm-1990-05-05-vw-353-story.html.

Introduction

There didn't seem to be anything godly or wholesome about the "penalties" in what was called the Endowment Session, but we were taught we must go through this ritual if we expected to live with God the Father and our families for eternity.

It seemed like after I began attending the temple regularly that the demonic attacks returned and increased. I didn't understand why it was happening. I guessed it was evil spirits of some kind, but it wasn't anything that was ever discussed in church. I went to my ward (congregation) leaders for guidance, but they didn't know what it was or how to stop it, other than to pray more, spend more time reading The Book of Mormon, and attending the temple more frequently.

It came to my mind to start using the name of Jesus to make the episodes stop. When those moments of terror came, I would try with all my effort and strength to call out the name of Jesus. Sometimes I could manage to speak His name out loud, and other times only in my mind; but as soon as I was able to call on Jesus the demonic presence would leave.

I wondered if there was some hidden sin in me that I was not consciously aware of—something that would trigger these attacks. It seemed like the more righteous I tried to be, the more frequent they became. I had no clue that the temple ceremonies were occult in nature. I only knew that being "temple worthy" and seeking ways to grow spiritually was part of our progression toward godhood.

As Mormons, we believed that we were to grow spiritually and become more and more righteous until one day in the eternities we could become gods and goddesses of our own worlds.

A few months preceding my departure from Mormonism, I was invited to a special fireside meeting where a notable LDS speaker would be presenting a seminar on deepening our spiritual walk. I was excited to go because so many of my friends and other ward members were always telling me about some spiritual experience they had.

People can have supernatural experiences regardless of their religious beliefs. This is why it's so important to test the spirits (1 John 4:1) and know the word of God. My friends would tell me about the times they went to the temple and could feel the presence of their ancestors, or they would have some dream or vision, or a special prompting of the Holy

Ghost. I didn't understand why they were getting all these "warm fuzzy" manifestations, while it seemed as though the only spiritual experiences I was having were evil spirits visiting me at night.

At the seminar the guest speaker gave us various exercises to increase our sensitivity to "the Spirit" (referring to the Holy Ghost). One of the activities was called a connected-breathing exercise where we were to lie on the floor with our knees bent, breathe deeply and slowly with our eyes closed, and to empty our minds. Pretty soon everyone was having some spiritual experience except me. Some were having visions, some were laughing hysterically, others were sobbing uncontrollably, still others were moaning as if gripped in ecstasy.

Discouraged, I finally got up and did what any sensible person would do. I went to the kitchen, got myself a plateful of yummy treats, and sat down to watch the theatrics. After everyone's emotions were spent, we gathered in the living room to talk about our experiences during the exercise. When it was my turn, I explained that nothing happened to me. I felt like an outsider looking in and wondered what was wrong with me. Was I not worthy enough? Did I not have enough faith?

A month later God—the real God—put His plan to save me into motion. I didn't spend much time watching television (who has time when you're raising a big family), but a friend suggested I check out the Oprah Winfrey Show to apply to appear as a guest for a special segment she was doing. It was about getting a Frumpy Clothes Makeover and they were looking for guests to be on the show. I was an expert at frumpiness! Nine kids at the time, baggy clothes, worn-out shoes—I could do frumpy!

My daughter got out the camcorder (one of those ancient devices that weighed about 40 pounds and rested of your shoulder, and you could never take it anywhere fun unless you had a wheelbarrow to carry it) and recorded me singing a song I wrote called *The Frumpy Clothes Blues*. A few days after sending the VHS tape via FedEx, I got a phone call from one of Oprah's staff, "How would you like to come to Chicago?"

I ended up on Oprah, and February 11, 2000, the day the show aired, I got a phone call —a blast from the past—from someone I hadn't heard from in 20 years; my arch-enemy Becky! She and I had both been dating the same guy for four long, painful years before he could decide which one of us to marry (in the end he chose me, by the way).

Introduction

Becky said she saw me on Oprah and felt inspired to look me up. She had been a devout Mormon for as long as I knew her, and now she was telling me that she had left Mormonism and was a born-again Christian. I figured that God set this whole thing up so I could bring her back into the LDS Church. Ironically, it was the other way around. She called me every weekend all summer long to tell me about Jesus and how much she loved Him. She kept telling me how much she loved reading the Bible.

So, I started reading the New Testament to see what was so great about it and what was in it that would make Becky leave the LDS Church. I thought the Bible was boring, somewhat confusing, and certainly not reliable. We were taught that the Bible wasn't translated correctly and that many precious truths had been removed from it by corrupt priests and translators.

That was the beginning of my search for truth. I didn't know how this came to mind (although looking back I now see it was the Holy Spirit), but I addressed my prayer specifically to the God of Abraham, Isaac, and Jacob. My line of thinking was such; if the Mormon gospel is true, then the God of Abraham, Isaac, and Jacob would be the God of Mormonism. But if it isn't true, I wanted to be certain my prayers were going to the real God of the universe. This is what I prayed; "I want to know the truth even if it means I've been wrong all my life."

A few weeks later, I came across information and documents that proved Mormonism wasn't true. I gave my life to Jesus November of 2000. All the thrilling details are in my book, *Mormonism, the Matrix, and Me* (shameless plug). Within weeks of getting saved, I was healed of debilitating back pain I had suffered from for years. Life was sweet. I could hardly put the Bible down. The book I once thought was boring and difficult to understand became the most exciting book I had ever read! Going to church became a privilege and a joy instead of a necessary obligation and burden.

I thought that the demonic was out of my life forever, and it did disappear for a few years. But then the attacks of so-called sleep paralysis began again. It wasn't often, and it felt different than before I was saved. When I was Mormon, I could sense or feel like the evil entities were trying to get inside me. This time it was like they knew they couldn't possess me; they could only try to scare and harass me.

Before being saved, it would happen just as I was falling asleep. After being saved, it would happen as I was waking up or in the middle of the night after first having a demonic dream. This is not to say that everyone experiencing attacks has it happen the same way. Vicki Joy Anderson's book, *They Only Come Out at Night*, goes into great depth about this phenomenon. I've observed that when I pray before going to sleep, asking for God to protect me and set His holy angels around me, that I sleep peacefully and soundly.

These experiences have done a couple things. First, they've strengthened my faith in God. Because I've experienced a glimpse of the powers of darkness—which operates in an inter-dimensional kingdom of falsehood, torment, and death—I'm confident that God is exists, and His Kingdom is one of light, life, and truth. Second, it led me into learning about spiritual warfare and taking steps to become trained in it.

Spiritual warfare isn't about a special technique or gift, it's knowing who you are in Christ Jesus and understanding the authority He gives us to act in His name. We were born into a war that rages between the forces of good and evil. It's our task to don the armor of God and walk the walk of a warrior.

1
How the Battle Began

*And there was war in heaven, Michael and his angels waging war
with the dragon. The dragon and his angels waged war,
and they did not prevail, and there was no longer a place found
for them in heaven. And the great dragon was thrown down,
the serpent of old who is called the devil and Satan, who deceives
the whole world; he was thrown down to the earth,
and his angels were thrown down with him...
Woe to the earth and the sea, because the devil has come down to
you with great wrath, knowing that he has only a short time.
Revelation 12:7–9, 12*

The warrior's walk is one of circumspection, soberness, and diligence, considering the time in which we live. Why an emphasis on holiness? Reasons are abundant, but in terms of spiritual warfare it's imperative. Here is the short account. "Long ago, in a galaxy near to us," prior to the creation of our first parents Adam and Eve, a great rebellion took place in the heavenlies. Lucifer became full of himself, and in his pride drew away a third of the host of heaven.

Angels were God's first family, in a manner of speaking, and God predetermined to bring a new kind of being into the family circle—man. However, humans are created in God's image; angels are not.

Suffice it to say, a little bit of jealousy ensued. It didn't sit well with Lucifer that God give dominion over the earth to these "lesser beings," and especially that he was appointed to be subservient to the humans Yahweh had placed in the garden of Eden. Through a cunning act of usurpation, Lucifer "legally" obtained the deed to Planet Earth.

The Almighty could have just "poofed" Satan and his followers out of existence. He had the power to do so, but that would go against His character and nature. Being omniscient, God preconceived a marvelous plan—a mystery in regard to restoring mankind, so that "in the ages to come" (Ephesians 2:7) His compassion, goodness, mercy, and justice would be manifest throughout all eternity.

Satan stood (and still stands) as the Accuser, the Father of Lies, the Slanderer. And he slandered God's great name. He characterized God as a tyrant, a selfish and power-hungry Being whose only thought was to be worshiped and take glory for Himself.

It was "unfair," Satan rationalized, that he—the most beautiful, wise, and powerful of all the angelic host—should be reduced to a servant in the household of God. Satan was full of unbridled pride, so much so, that every thought of evil dominated his thinking at all times. He was persuasive enough to convince a third of angelic beings to rebel against God, and he and his army of followerrs have been out to destroy humanity and exact revenge on the Creator ever since.

The first several verses of Genesis 6 tells about the Benei Elohim, the sons of God who came down from their heavenly abode to have sexual relations with human women. It wasn't simply a matter of lust; their goal was to corrupt the human gene pool and thereby retain "ownership" of the earth. A full account of what occurred can be found in the first book of Enoch. A well-written and condensed version of this account is in an article on Torah.com, excerpted below:

> The result of this union is unnatural, as could be expected: the women bear violent giants. The giants' violence and voracious hunger cause humans tremendous distress, as well as setting off a "domino effect" of violence among all creatures of the world.

The final result of all this illicit angelic intervention is the Flood, either to rid the world of contamination or to end the humans' sin.

In this third version of the story, the giants themselves are killed. Their spirits, however, deriving from immortal heavenly beings (the angels), cannot be destroyed completely, but also cannot return to heaven. They remain connected to earth as evil spirits, wreaking havoc among humankind and causing both physical evil (such as disease) and moral evil (sin):

> [Enoch] *7:8 And now the giants who were born from spirits and flesh will be called evil spirits upon the earth, and on the earth will be their dwelling.*
> *7:9 And evil spirits came out from their flesh because from above they were created; from the holy Watchers was their origin and first foundation. Evil spirits they will be on the earth, and spirits of the evil ones they will be called.*
> *7:10 And the dwelling of the spirits of heaven is in heaven, but the dwelling of the spirits of earth, who were born on the earth, [is] on earth.*
> *7:11 And the spirits of the giants . . . which do wrong and are corrupt, and attack and fight and break on the earth, and cause sorrow; and they eat no food and do not thirst, and are not observed.*
> *7:12 And these spirits will rise against the sons of men and against the women because they came out [from them] (Brand, 2016).*[1]

Since Yahweh is a God of order, holiness, and perfection, He will not violate His own principles and laws. Thus, the King's courtyard becomes a court of law, with Satan as the prosecuting attorney and man as the defendant. God loved His creation, and thus in order to save

---

1. Miryam Brand, "The Benei Elohim, the Watchers, and the Origins of Evil" TheTorah.com (2016). https://thetorah.com/article/the-benei-elohim-the-watchers-and-the-origins-of-evil.

humanity, He came down in human form to pay the penalty for man's sin. It caught Satan and the fallen ones completely off guard!

> **1 Corinthians 2:6–10 (TLV)**
> *We do speak wisdom, however, among those who are mature—but not a wisdom of this age or of the rulers of this age, who are coming to nothing. Rather, we speak God's wisdom in a mystery—a wisdom that has been hidden, which God destined for our glory before the ages.* **None of the rulers of this age understood it—for if they had, they would not have crucified the Lord of glory.** *[Emphasis mine.]*

As it is, the battle rages on. The forces of darkness are powerful and unrelenting. And while humanity is being assaulted on all fronts, it's the redeemed who are the main focus of Satan's wrath. You and I are on the "hit list," with demonic spiritual assassins assigned to take us out. Thank God for His protection and ever watchful eyes! And thankfully we have scores of His holy angels around us to stand guard and to fight.

> **2 Kings 6:15-17**
> *Now when the attendant of the man of God had risen early and gone out, behold, an army with horses and chariots was circling the city. And his servant said to him, "This is hopeless, my master! What are we to do?"*
>
> *And he said, "Do not be afraid, for those who are with us are greater than those who are with them." Then Elisha prayed and said, "Lord, please, open his eyes so that he may see." And the Lord opened the servant's eyes, and he saw; and behold, the mountain was full of horses and chariots of fire all around Elisha.*

Thus, we must be attired in the armor God has provided. Our Father in heaven is not legalistic: "strict, literal, or excessive conformity to the law or to a religious or moral code" (Merriam-Webster.com), but demons and fallen angels are. They will use every legal loophole possible to infiltrate our lives to harass and oppress us.

That's why, for example, dabbling in the occult, reading one's daily horoscope, unforgiveness (this is a big one), sin, using mind-altering substances, etc., give an opening for demonic activity in your life. The devil doesn't say, "Oh, Tommy was only five when he was playing with the Ouija Board and he thought it was just a game, so he gets a free pass." Or "Sally was treated horribly by her brother growing up; she has good cause to hold it against him; so I'll leave her alone."

Fallen angels and demons don't have *any* compassion or empathy at all. They hate us with every fiber of their being. They're totally incapable of feeling sorrow or mercy. They're full of rage. They're conniving. They never sleep or rest. They are committed to our destruction. Therefore, we cannot be lackadaisical in our walk with God or in wearing the armor. But we need not fear if we are walking the walk:

Psalm 91
One who dwells in the shelter of the Most High
Will lodge in the shadow of the Almighty.
I will say to the Lord, "My refuge and my fortress,
My God, in whom I trust!"
For it is He who rescues you from the net of the trapper
And from the deadly plague.
He will cover you with His pinions,
And under His wings you may take refuge;
His faithfulness is a shield and wall.
You will not be afraid of the terror by night,
Or of the arrow that flies by day;
Of the plague that stalks in darkness,
Or of the destruction that devastates at noon.
A thousand may fall at your side
And ten thousand at your right hand,
But it shall not approach you.
You will only look on with your eyes
And see the retaliation against the wicked.
For you have made the Lord, my refuge,

The Warrior's Walk

The Most High, your dwelling place.
No evil will happen to you,
Nor will any plague come near your tent.
For He will give His angels orders concerning you,
To protect you in all your ways.
On their hands they will lift you up,
So that you do not strike your foot against a stone.
You will walk upon the lion and cobra,
You will trample the young lion and the serpent.
"Because he has loved Me, I will save him;
I will set him securely on high, because he has known My name.
He will call upon Me, and I will answer him;
I will be with him in trouble;
I will rescue him and honor him.
I will satisfy him with a long life,
And show him My salvation."

2

Our Identity in Messiah

Therefore if anyone is in Christ, he is a new creature; the old things passed away; behold, new things have come.
2 Corinthians 5:17

In the Hebrew Scriptures (the Old Testament) the tale of Mephibosheth unfolds. He was the grandson of King Saul and son of David's close friend, Jonathan. Crippled since childhood, Mephibosheth, though Jonathan's son, remained unknown to King David for a time:

> **2 Samuel 4:4**
> *Now Jonathan, Saul's son, had a son crippled in his feet. He was five years old when the report of Saul and Jonathan came from Jezreel, and his nurse took him up and fled. And it happened that in her hurry to flee, he fell and became lame. And his name was Mephibosheth.*

In the culture of that time, David could easily have been expected to put Mephibosheth to death, but despite potential rivalry due to his lineage, David, in a remarkable show of mercy and kindness, showered him with gifts, treating him like family and granting him Saul's estate.

David's actions stemmed from a covenant with Jonathan, the Crown Prince who yielded his claim to the throne for David, anointed by the prophet Samuel. David's kindness toward Mephibosheth sprang out of the love he had for his best friend Jonathan, This unique pact led to David's unconditional blessings upon Mephibosheth. Let's take a deeper dive into the account:

2 Samuel 9:1–11
Then David said, "Is there yet anyone left of the house of Saul, that I may show him kindness for Jonathan's sake?"
Now there was a servant of the house of Saul whose name was Ziba, and they called him to David; and the king said to him, "Are you Ziba?" And he said, "I am your servant."
The king said, "Is there not yet anyone of the house of Saul to whom I may show the kindness of God?" And Ziba said to the king, "There is still a son of Jonathan who is crippled in both feet."
So the king said to him, "Where is he?" And Ziba said to the king, "Behold, he is in the house of Machir the son of Ammiel in Lo-debar."
Then King David sent and brought him from the house of Machir the son of Ammiel, from Lo-debar.
Mephibosheth, the son of Jonathan the son of Saul, came to David and fell on his face and prostrated himself. And David said, "Mephibosheth." And he said, "Here is your servant!"
David said to him, "Do not fear, for I will surely show kindness to you for the sake of your father Jonathan, and will restore to you all the land of your grandfather Saul; and you shall eat at my table regularly."
Again he prostrated himself and said, "What is your servant, that you should regard a dead dog like me?"
Then the king called Saul's servant Ziba and said to him, "All that belonged to Saul and to all his house I have given to your master's grandson.

> *You and your sons and your servants shall cultivate the land for him, and you shall bring in the produce so that your master's grandson may have food; nevertheless Mephibosheth your master's grandson shall eat at my table regularly." Now Ziba had fifteen sons and twenty servants.*
>
> *Then Ziba said to the king, "According to all that my lord the king commands his servant so your servant will do." So Mephibosheth ate at David's table as one of the king's sons.*

The story parallels God's grace through Christ, emphasizing that spiritual blessings come freely, not earned by our actions. The narrative is instructive because it highlights God's lavish blessings that we have in Jesus, mirroring David's generosity to Mephibosheth. As believers in covenant with God, we receive abundant blessings, and look forward to an extravagant and generous inheritance as Jesus' bride and children of the Kingdom. Paul's teachings echo this divine plan—a family created from all nations, united through Jesus as the central connection, aligning heaven and earth under his leadership.

The apostle Paul wrote, "Blessed be the God and Father of our Lord Jesus Christ, who has blessed us in Christ with every spiritual blessing in the heavenly places" (Ephesians 1:3). God predestined these blessings for those in Christ, revealing an eternal plan to redeem mankind. Despite opposition, God's victory at the cross ensures the fulfillment of His plans. In Messiah, we possess everything God desires for us at the conclusion of His judgment against the kingdom of darkness.

Satan and his hosts will do everything they can to kill, steal, and destroy; and that includes killing, stealing, and destroying our identities. We see this happening on several fronts. Our bodies are being attacked through GMO foods, mRNA technologies, transhumanism, nano particles, chemtrails, and other poisons. His desire is to change our DNA because it has God's imprint on it.

The Enemy attacks, as well, by casting doubt on who we are in the Kingdom of Light; we are children of the Most High God and heirs in His kingdom! Before salvation we were "in Adam," and as such were subject to the curses and judgments pronounced on all his descendants. After being redeemed and brought under the new covenant of Jesus' blood, we are "in Christ," and beneficiaries of all the blessings that come from being bonded to Him through the new covenant and the Holy Spirit.

Concerning Ephesians 1:3, that God has "blessed us in Christ with every spiritual blessing in the heavenly places," we need to keep in mind that these are spiritual blessings. It isn't until God restores His kingdom to the earth that we receive all of the physical and material blessings He has in store for us.

As for now, we live in a broken world. Our bodies are frail and subject to illness. But an age is coming when all the blessings our Father and King has for us will be bestowed upon His sons and daughters. Paul points out many of the spiritual blessings that are ours in Christ now:

Chosen
Just as He chose us in Him before the foundation of the world, that we would be holy and blameless before Him (Eph. 1:4).

Adopted
In love He predestined us to adoption as sons through Jesus Christ to Himself, according to the kind intention of His will, to the praise of the glory of His grace, which He freely bestowed on us in the Beloved (Eph. 1:5–6).

Redeemed and Forgiven
In Him we have redemption through His blood, the forgiveness of our trespasses, according to the riches of His grace which He lavished on us (Eph. 1:7–8).

Given an Inheritance
In Him also we have obtained an inheritance, having been predestined according to His purpose who works all things after the counsel of His will, to the end that we who were the first to hope in Christ would be to the praise of His glory (Eph. 1:11–12).

Sealed with the Holy Spirit
In Him, you also, after listening to the message of truth, the gospel of your salvation—having also believed, you were sealed in Him with the Holy Spirit of promise, who is given as a pledge of our inheritance, with a view to the redemption of God's own possession, to the praise of His glory (Eph. 1:13–14).

In the realm of spiritual blessings bestowed upon believers through the new covenant, these spiritual endowments are ours through a legal transaction executed by God. He has generously granted more than we can fathom, irrespective of our deserving. Paul's teachings reveal God's eternal plan to unite a diverse earthly family with the heavenly one, anchored in the connection through Jesus.

Hebrews 6:17–20
In the same way God wanted to demonstrate more clearly to the heirs of the promise that his purpose was unchangeable, and so he intervened with an oath, so that we who have found refuge in him may find strong encouragement to hold fast to the hope set before us through two unchangeable things, since it is impossible for God to lie.

We have this hope as an anchor for the soul, sure and steadfast, which reaches inside behind the curtain, where Jesus our forerunner entered on our behalf, since he became a priest forever in the order of Melchizedek.

We can see why Satan and the demonic realm would want believers to get discouraged, and where possible to give up.

Daniel 7:25
And he shall speak great words against the Most High and shall wear out the saints of the most High.

Satan attacks directly when necessary, and uses asymmetric warfare when he can't launch a direct assault; meaning he will use indirect tactics to exhaust the strength of and demoralize the resolve of believers.

I would venture that most professing Christians really don't know their identity in Christ. They understand they are children of God, but only have a vague idea of what that means.

Satan does everything he can to discredit God and malign His character. But who is the one that kills, steals, and destroys? Who is the one who is the source of suffering, disease, misery, and sorrow? Satan. He brings these things to the table, and then when humans experience them, he whispers, "It's God's fault. How could a loving God allow these things to happen? He doesn't love you. He's doesn't care."

Or he'll directly attack a Christian's identity by whispering, "I know all about you. You're a screw-up. You've gone too far. God could never forgive you for doing what you've done. Oh, how you stumbled! It just shows you're not worthy of the Father's love."

But when you comprehend that *your* identity is *Christ's* identity, there's power in that! We are clothed in Jesus' righteousness. We are joint heirs with Him. We can be confident in His promises.

Isaiah 49:13–16

Sing, heaven! Rejoice, earth!
Break out in song, you mountains!
For Adonai (the LORD) is comforting his people,
having mercy on his own who have suffered.
"But Tziyon (Zion) says, 'Adonai has abandoned me,
Adonai has forgotten me.'
Can a woman forget her child at the breast,
not show pity on the child from her womb?
Even if these were to forget,
I would not forget you.
I have engraved you on the palms of my hands,
your walls are always before me."

Although this passage of Scripture is referring specifically to Israel, the heart of God is the same toward us. Our circumstances are always in front of Him. He has not forgotten you. He has not forgotten me. The time is coming when all things will be set right. But until then, we will need to endure much. There are difficult days ahead of us, and if we are not sure of our identity in Jesus as heirs of His kingdom, we'll become casualties on the battlefield.

These verses serve as reminders of our heritage as children of God:

1 Corinthians 3:16
Do you not know that you are a temple of God and that the Spirit of God dwells in you?

1 Corinthians 6:19
Or do you not know that your body is a temple of the Holy Spirit within you, whom you have from God, and that you are not your own? For you have been bought for a price: therefore glorify God in your body.

Ephesians 2:19–22
So then, you are no longer foreigners and strangers. On the contrary, you are fellow-citizens with God's people and members of God's family. You have been built on the foundation of the apostles and the prophets, with the cornerstone being Yeshua the Messiah himself.

In union with him the whole building is held together, and it is growing into a holy temple in union with the Lord. Yes, in union with him, you yourselves are being built together into a spiritual dwelling-place for God!

Colossians 2:9-10
See to it that there is no one who takes you captive through philosophy and empty deception in accordance with human tradition, in accordance with the elementary principles of the world, rather than in accordance with Christ. For in Him all the fullness of Deity dwells in bodily form, and in Him you have been made complete, and He is the head over every ruler and authority…

I love this passage in 2 Corinthians 5:15–21 (CJB):

> *So from now on, we do not look at anyone from a worldly viewpoint. Even if we once regarded the Messiah from a worldly viewpoint, we do so no longer. Therefore, if anyone is united with the Messiah, he is a new creation—the old has passed; look, what has come is fresh and new!*
>
> *And it is all from God, who through the Messiah has reconciled us to himself and has given us the work of that reconciliation, which is that God in the Messiah was reconciling mankind to himself, not counting their sins against them, and entrusting to us the message of reconciliation.*
>
> *Therefore, we are ambassadors of the Messiah; in effect, God is making his appeal through us. What we do is appeal on behalf of the Messiah, "Be reconciled to God! God made this sinless man be a sin offering on our behalf, so that in union with him we might fully share in God's righteousness."*

And so we see that spiritual warfare is not limited to casting out demons. It isn't restricted to inner healing and deliverance ministries. Life itself is spiritual warfare. When we daily walk in our identities as sons and daughters of the Living God, knowing that our inheritance awaits us, and using the spiritual weapons that have been entrusted to us, we *can* and *will* overcome the Enemy.

3

Authority of the Believer

Remember, I have given you authority; so you can trample down snakes and scorpions, indeed, all the Enemy's forces; and you will remain completely unharmed.
Luke 10:19

In his classic work *The Authority of The Believer*, John A. Macmillan wrote about an subject which holds true today;

> There are few subjects relating to the Christian life concerning which there is so little exact knowledge as that of the authority of the believer. This is not because such authority is the property only of a few elect souls. On the contrary, it is the possession of every true child of God. It is one of the "all things" received in Christ. Its reception dates from the soul's contact with Calvary.
>
> Probably because of the extreme importance of a correct understanding of its privileges and responsibilities, and because of the power which they confer on a militant believer, the enemy has specially sought to hold back this

knowledge from God's people. He has been successful through the employment of the "blinding" tactics which he has found effective in the case of the "lost" and of those who "believe not" (2 Cor. 4:3, 4). For it is strangely true that, although its principles are set forth in a definite way in this epistle to the Ephesians, there is very little grasp in the majority of even spiritual believers."

The authority of the believer is by some confounded with the fullness of the Spirit. It is taught that the coming of the gracious Spirit of God into the soul in His divine fullness gives authority. But the believer's authority exists before he seeks or realizes in any special way the Spirit's presence. It is certainly true that the fullness of the Spirit empowers and enlightens the believer. By this alone he is enabled to exercise authority. But the fullness is not the source of the authority, but something apart from it.[1] (Macmillan 1932, 1)

As God's redeemed people, we're invited to participate in building His kingdom and carrying out His purpose for mankind. If we're to join Him in advancing His mission, we need to know and understand what the mission is. Quoting from the scroll of Isaiah in the synagogue in Nazareth, Jesus identified His purpose:

Luke 4:18
The Spirit of the Lord is upon Me,
Because He anointed Me to preach the gospel to the poor.
He has sent Me to proclaim release to the captives,
And recovery of sight to the blind,
To set free those who are oppressed,
To proclaim the favorable year of the Lord.

---

1. Macmillan, John A. 1932. The Authority of the Believer. Grapevine India. https://www.amazon.com/gp/product/B09ZV76Q9B/.

Jesus spoke with such authority and power that it prompted questions about the possibility of His Messiahship. Yet, He attributed His actions to the Father, fully embodying both divinity and humanity. His supernatural works didn't spring from His deity, but from the authority given to Him as a man by God.

Philippians 2:6–7 (NLT)
You must have the same attitude that Christ Jesus had.
Though he was God,
  he did not think of equality with God
  as something to cling to.
Instead, he gave up his divine privileges;
  he took the humble position of a slave
  and was born as a human being.
When he appeared in human form,
  he humbled himself in obedience to God
  and died a criminal's death on a cross.
Therefore, God elevated him to the place of highest honor
  and gave him the name above all other names,
that at the name of Jesus every knee should bow,
  in heaven and on earth and under the earth,
and every tongue declare that Jesus Christ is Lord,
  to the glory of God the Father.

Jesus did nothing on His own authority, but did only what He saw His Father doing:

John 5:19, 30
Therefore Jesus answered and was saying to them, "Truly, truly, I say to you, the Son can do nothing of Himself, unless it is something He sees the Father doing; for whatever the Father does, these things the Son also does in like manner...

I can do nothing on My own initiative. As I hear, I judge; and My judgment is just, because I do not seek My own will, but the will of Him who sent Me.

Luke 5:17–26:
One day He was teaching; and there were some Pharisees and teachers of the law sitting there, who had come from every village of Galilee and Judea and from Jerusalem; and the power of the Lord was present for Him to perform healing. And some men were carrying on a bed a man who was paralyzed; and they were trying to bring him in and to set him down in front of Him. But not finding any way to bring him in because of the crowd, they went up on the roof and let him down through the tiles with his stretcher, into the middle of the crowd, in front of Jesus.

Seeing their faith, He said, "Friend, your sins are forgiven you." The scribes and the Pharisees began to reason, saying, "Who is this man who speaks blasphemies? Who can forgive sins, but God alone?" But Jesus, aware of their reasonings, answered and said to them, "Why are you reasoning in your hearts? Which is easier, to say, 'Your sins have been forgiven you,' or to say, 'Get up and walk'? But, so that you may know that the Son of Man has authority on earth to forgive sins,"—He said to the paralytic—"I say to you, get up, and pick up your stretcher and go home."

Immediately he got up before them, and picked up what he had been lying on, and went home glorifying God. They were all struck with astonishment and began glorifying God; and they were filled with fear, saying, "We have seen remarkable things today."

Jesus is our teacher, our rabbi. He demonstrated to His disciples then, and now to us, how we are to do kingdom work on the earth. An important key to doing this is to establish a close relationship to our Father in Heaven and develop intimacy with Him. This comes through praying, spending time in the Word, walking in His ways, eliminating distractions, and coming out from Babylon—the world system of behavior, practice, and thought.

Luke 5:16 explains that Jesus would often "slip away to the wilderness and pray." For those living in a city it may be a challenge to get away to the "wilderness." Still, slipping away to pray might be sitting alone in your vehicle, sitting on the back porch or deck, taking a walk, or secluding yourself in your bedroom before the family awakens or after the children are tucked in bed.

When we take the time to hear His voice, the Holy Spirit will instruct and guide us into what we should do. Perhaps someone has a specific need to be filled, or someone needs prayer or encouragement. We must be prepared and ready to serve at God's calling. The greater our obedience, the more He can trust us with bigger responsibilities:

> **Luke 16:10**
> *The one who is faithful in a very little thing is also faithful in much; and the one who is unrighteous in a very little thing is also unrighteous in much.*

The Western church is weak, my friends. The status quo of many modern professing Christians can be characterized as being "lovers of pleasure [entertainment] rather than lovers of God, holding to a form of godliness although they have denied its power" (2 Timothy 3:4–5, brackets mine).

This is not how it should be! Jesus is the prototype of "normal." In general, we give lip service to Matthew 10:8; *"Heal the sick, raise the dead, cure those with leprosy, and cast out demons,"* but are we doing it? I have friends and family members who went as missionaries to other countries and operated in a Matthew 10:8 capacity. They've seen miracles with their own eyes: the lame made whole, the blind see, the deaf receive hearing, and yes—even the dead being raised to life (freshly dead, not like already rotting in the grave).

Is this authority and power reserved only for those abroad? No! It is ours too. But we have to get off our spiritual rear-ends, live uprightly before God, develop intimacy with Him to the point we know His will and can act on it, and then *move forward in trust and confidence.* Jesus said:

> **John 14:12–14 (NLT)**
> *I tell you the truth, anyone who believes in me will do the same*

works I have done, and even greater works, because I am going to be with the Father. You can ask for anything in my name, and I will do it, so that the Son can bring glory to the Father. Yes, ask me for anything in my name, and I will do it!

Jesus' ministry was an overflow of His intimacy and communion with His Father. It's sometimes difficul to imagine doing the works Jesus did, and even greater; but we need to realize that He gave us the authority to do so. Rabbi Jesus chose 12 men to be in His inner circle of students, and after some time, He sent them out on their own:

Luke 9:1–2
Now He called the twelve together and gave them power and authority over all the demons, and the power to heal diseases. And He sent them out to proclaim the kingdom of God and to perform healing.

Jesus had many followers and disciples outside His inner circle of 12. In fact, He sent 70 of them out on assignment:[2]

Luke 10:1–2 (CJB)
After this, the Lord appointed seventy other talmidim [disciples, students] and sent them on ahead in pairs to every town and place where he himself was about to go.

---

2. Some Bible versions say 70, while others say 72. From GotQuestions.org; "The discrepancies in the number (70 or 72) come from differences found in approximately half of the ancient scrolls used in translation. The texts are nearly evenly divided between the numbers, and scholars do not agree on whether the number should be 70 or 72, although such a minor issue is no cause for debate. Since the number 70 is repeated other places in Scripture (Exodus 24:1; Numbers 11:16; Jeremiah 29:10), it may be more likely that the actual number of disciples was 70, with the 2 being a copyist's error." (Retrieved from https://www.gotquestions.org/70-or-72-disciples.html).

Biblically, the number 70 symbolizes comprehensiveness. It also represents the 70 nations as determined at the tower of Babel.

He said to them, "To be sure, there is a large harvest. But there are few workers. Therefore, plead with the Lord of the Harvest that he speed workers out to gather in his harvest.

Luke 10:17–20 (CJB)
The seventy came back jubilant. "Lord," they said, "with your power, even the demons submit to us!"

Yeshua said to them, "I saw Satan fall like lightning from heaven. Remember, I have given you authority; so you can trample down snakes and scorpions, indeed, all the Enemy's forces; and you will remain completely unharmed.

Nevertheless, don't be glad that the spirits submit to you; be glad that your names have been recorded in heaven."

The men who were sent out ahead of Jesus to prepare the way did wonders in His name, and as He promised, they were unharmed by the forces of evil. Contrarily, the "seven sons of Sceva" actually *were* harmed! They spoke in Jesus' name, but they didn't have His authority:

Acts 19:13–16
But also some of the Jewish exorcists, who went from place to place, attempted to use the name of the Lord Jesus over those who had the evil spirits, saying, "I order you in the name of Jesus whom Paul preaches!"

Now there were seven sons of Sceva, a Jewish chief priest, doing this. But the evil spirit responded and said to them, "I recognize Jesus, and I know of Paul, but who are you?" And the man in whom was the evil spirit, pounced on them and subdued all of them and overpowered them, so that they fled out of that house naked and wounded.

There is power in the name of Jesus, but only those who are born-again from above have the authority to act in His name. This authority is demonstrated in the Great Commssion, which Jesus instructed His disciples to carry out:

> **Matthew 28:18–20**
> *And Jesus came up and spoke to them, saying, "All authority in heaven and on earth has been given to Me. Go, therefore, and make disciples of all the nations, baptizing them in the name of the Father and the Son and the Holy Spirit, teaching them to follow all that I commanded you; and behold, I am with you always, to the end of the age."*

Jesus entrusted His ministry to us, leaving us in charge of the Kingdom on earth. He is the archetype of what a Kingdom Warrior is supposed to be. He demonstrated what the life of a citizen of heaven should be like. We were not intended to be bystanders, but to be participants acting as the hands and feet of our King. *His* ministry is *our* ministry—the "family business" passed down from Father to Son to us.

The book of Acts showcases believers executing Jesus' commission, revealing the power and authority passed on to them. Since that time, down through the last two millennia to the present, God's miracles have occurred worldwide. Reports are made of healings, the blind given sight, the hearing to the deaf, the crippled made whole, the dead brought back to life, and *most* importantly, souls being delivered from the kingdom of darkness into the Kingdom of Light. These miracles done in the mighty name of Jesus are being witnessed by believers and unbelievers alike in even the remotest parts of the earth, debunking misconceptions about miracles ending with the death of the apostles, and emphasizing the importance of aligning our beliefs with Scripture.

The accounts of Peter, John, Philip, Stephen, and Paul are among the many amazing works God performed through these faithful men, which shows that authority, power, and miracles were not consigned only to the time period Jesus' walked the earth. The Lord did not withdraw His authority from His followers when He returned to His Father's throne.

> **Acts 3:1–8**
> *Now Peter and John were going up to the temple at the ninth*

hour, the hour of prayer. And a man who had been unable to walk from birth was being carried, whom they used to set down every day at the gate of the temple which is called Beautiful, in order for him to beg for charitable gifts from those entering the temple grounds.

When he saw Peter and John about to go into the temple grounds, he began asking to receive a charitable gift. But Peter, along with John, looked at him intently and said, "Look at us!" And he gave them his attention, expecting to receive something from them.

But Peter said, "I do not have silver and gold, but what I do have I give to you: In the name of Jesus Christ the Nazarene, walk!" And grasping him by the right hand, he raised him up; and immediately his feet and his ankles were strengthened. And leaping up, he stood and began to walk; and he entered the temple with them, walking and leaping and praising God.

Acts 6:8
And Stephen, full of grace and power, was performing great wonders and signs among the people.

Acts 8:4–8
Philip went down to the city of Samaria and began proclaiming Christ to them. The crowds with one accord were giving attention to what was said by Philip, as they heard and saw the signs which he was performing. For in the case of many who had unclean spirits, they were coming out of them shouting with a loud voice; and many who had been paralyzed and lame were healed. So there was much rejoicing in that city.

Tragically, those who are part of cultural Christianity or western mainstream churches have never witnessed the baptism of the Holy Spirit, healings, miracles, and the power of God. They've been led to believe that such things are not for today, and that their mission lies in "evangelism lite," ("Jesus loves you, and if he had a refrigerator, your picture would be on it!"). Blending in with the world and being liked has taken priority over obedience to the command to come out of Babylon.

Our task is aligning our will with Jesus, the Father, and the Holy Spirit, exercising the authority given to us. Our authority, received upon becoming children of God, doesn't require pursuit—it requires acknowledgement and proper use. The enemy attacks our God-given authority through self-image and doubt, hindering us from realizing our potential. Understanding our identity in Christ puts the kingdom of darkness in jeopardy.

It's imperative that we know who we are in Jesus and that we have an unshakable faith in the authority He gives each of us. We must understand that our identity is firmly established in our Messiah, Jesus, and in Him alone. We are not to just be on the sidelines or in the stands watching the game on the field. Jesus prayed this:

John 17:15–18
I don't ask you to take them out of the world, but to protect them from the Evil One. They do not belong to the world, just as I do not belong to the world. Set them apart for holiness by means of the truth — your word is truth. Just as you sent me into the world, I have sent them into the world.

Jesus gives us the right to use his authority according to His will:

1 John 5:14–15
This is the confidence which we have before Him, that, if we ask anything according to His will, He hears us. And if we know that He hears us in whatever we ask, we know that we have the requests which we have asked from Him.

Jesus acted on the Father's authority. He didn't ask the Father to heal someone or to cast demons out of the demonized; He used the authority given Him and directly commanded these things to be done. Of course, it isn't wrong for us to make requests of God and to ask Jesus to do something for us—to heal someone who is sick or suffering as we pray for them. But if we are listening to the Holy Spirit and are in alignment with His will, we can directly act in Jesus' name and command the healing or the casting out of a demon.

With permission, I share the miracle Jamie Walden of *Omega Dynamics Ministries* witnessed with the injury of his 11-year-old son. Jamie and his son Finley ran an errand to town together. While his dad was in the bank, Finley decided to climb a tree in a planter between the curb and the sidewalk.

Suddenly, Jamie heard a scream and ran outside to find his boy crumpled on the cement where he had fallen from a height of about 12- to 15 feet. Rushed to the hospital, Finley was diagnosed with a fractured skull—penetrating into the dura mater of his brain—and two fractured vertebrae.

Once Finley's body was stabilized in a brace, the doctors decided to wait a day before having him airlifted to Denver to see a pediatric specialist. Jamie and his wife opted to bring their son home for the night where they could tend to him before taking him back to the emergency room to be flown to Denver. Jamie describes the pain and suffering Finley was experiencing as he slipped in and out of consciousness.

Jamie and his wife had been praying fervently for their son, but just before carrying him out to the truck to transport him to the hospital for the life-flight to Denver, they stopped to pray over him one more time before the trip. Kneeling by Finley's side as he lie on the sofa writhing in agony, Jamie laid across him sobbing and asking the Lord to heal his son. Then—as clear as day—Jamie heard in his spirit the Lord firmly say, "Stop praying for Me to heal your son. *You* heal him. I've given you all that you need to do it."

Shocked, Jamie could hardly grasp what that even meant. He knew that some people try to manipulate God and speak out of their own desires rather than what the Holy Spirit is saying. He didn't want to put the Lord to the test.

Finally, after about 10 minutes of wrestling within himself, wanting to be obedient and yet fearing God, Jamie spoke these words, "Finley, you are healed in the name of Jesus Christ."

One of Finley's favorite worship songs was playing softly in the background, and over the following several minutes, he began "squeaking out sounds" (as his parents described it), and he began to audibly say the lyrics to the music based on Psalm 91. After the fourth time through the worship song, Finley sat up, vomited a few times, and then smiled, "Mama, I feel better now. All the pain is gone."

The Walden's testimony of this harrowing-turned-miraculous event can be found on YouTube[1], where Jamie goes into greater detail about going to the orthopedic surgeon's office with Finley and new x-rays showed a perfect spine and skull with no evidence of trauma or injury. Finley had been completely made whole by the power of the Living God! Under the direction of the Holy Spirit, Jamie used the authority he'd been given to heal his son.

Our authority, received through the Holy Spirit's indwelling, holds the full-strength power of Jesus. *We* are the limiting factor, not God, as evidenced in Jesus' teachings on faith. We offer our mustard seed of faith, trusting that God will use it to do mighty miracles and wonders. Empowered by the Holy Spirit, we're called to step up and live as God intended.

Facing the enemy, our authority and power reflect Jesus, supported by His everlasting presence. Our weaknesses lead us to rely on God's strength, reframing them as a means of dependence. Paul wrote to the saints in Corinth about his weakness, a "thorn in the flesh," that reminds us of our dependence on God;

> **2 Corinthians 12:7–10**
> *Because of the surpassing greatness of the revelations, for this reason, to keep me from exalting myself, there was given me a thorn in the flesh, a messenger of Satan to torment me—to keep me from exalting myself!*
>
> *Concerning this I implored the Lord three times that it might leave me. And He has said to me, "My grace is sufficient for you, for power is perfected in weakness."*

---

1. https://www.youtube.com/watch?v=m95X8h-L8jM

> *Most gladly, therefore, I will rather boast about my weaknesses, so that the power of Christ may dwell in me. Therefore I am well content with weaknesses, with insults, with distresses, with persecutions, with difficulties, for Christ's sake; for when I am weak, then I am strong.*

As royal ambassadors, we mirror Jesus' authority, speaking as if God Himself is communicating. Similar to earthly ambassadors, we need an understanding of heaven's culture, speaking with top-down authority. Our eternal authority, rooted in God's omnipotence, comes with the responsibilities of ambassadorship. Operating in God-given authority is critical for establishing His Kingdom on earth. Our citizenship is in God's eternal kingdom, and as temporary ambassadors, we wield authority that brings the weight of heaven into a lost world.

Unlike earthly rulers, our King's authority is eternal and unchanging, highlighting the perfect demonstration of His love. In realizing our identity and authority, we become conduits of heaven's influence on earth.

As John A. MacMillan penned;

> So, today, every consecrated hand that lifts the rod of the authority of the Lord against the unseen powers of darkness is directing the throne-power of Christ against Satan and his hosts in a battle that will last until "the going down of the sun," that is, until life's day is ended. (The Authority Of The Believer, 1932)

May we use the authority of the Lord with wisdom and love.

4

The Belt of Truth

Put on the full armor of God, so that you will be able to stand firm against the schemes of the devil. For our struggle is not against flesh and blood, but against the rulers, against the powers, against the world forces of this darkness, against the spiritual forces of wickedness in the heavenly places.
Ephesians 6:11–12

Some people say that the apostle Paul got his analogy about the armor of God by being chained to a Roman soldier, and that may very well be so. But the various pieces of armor are actually mentioned throughout the Bible. Here we see references to the belt as both part of one's armor and as a useful tool:

> **1 Samuel 18:4**
> *Jonathan stripped himself of the robe that was on him and gave it to David, with his armor, including his sword and his bow and **his belt**.*
>
> **2 Samuel 20:8**
> *When they were at the large stone which is in Gibeon, Amasa came to meet them. Now Joab was dressed in his military attire, and over it was **a belt** with a sword in its sheath fastened at*

his waist; and as he went forward, it fell out.

Psalm 109:19
*Let it be to him as a garment with which he covers himself, And for **a belt** with which he constantly girds himself.*

Daniel 2:5
*I lifted my eyes and looked, and behold, there was a certain man dressed in linen, whose waist was girded with **a belt** of pure gold of Uphaz.*

Matthew 3:4
*Now John himself had a garment of camel's hair and a leather **belt** around his waist; and his food was locusts and wild honey.*

Mark 6:8
*and He instructed them that they should take nothing for their journey, except a mere staff—no bread, no bag, no money in their **belt**—*

Acts 21:11
*And coming to us, he took Paul's belt and bound his own feet and hands, and said, "This is what the Holy Spirit says: 'In this way the Jews at Jerusalem will bind the man who owns this **belt** and deliver him into the hands of the Gentiles.'"*

Many times, you'll find Scripture describing the use of belts as "to gird up" one's loins. Since both men and women wore robes or long tunics in Israel in Bible times, belts were not used to hold up pants. Ancient Jews wore loose clothing, and they put on a girdle or belt only when going out to work or setting out to travel.

To gird up your loins means to prepare for action, and is used in the sense of encircling with a belt or a band. For utility purposes the sash or belt was used for tucking the bottom of one's robe into it so the robe didn't get in the way of running or working.

The belt was a utility tool, much like today's Leatherman multi-tool or cargo pants. Belts could be used to hang things from. Someone going to the market or on a journey might attach a leather pouch to their belt to carry coins.

By the time Rome was in power in Jesus' day, Roman soldiers used their belts to secure their daggers and hang other needed items on. Their swords were generally held by a shoulder strap called a "baldric," because it made for easier access when fighting. Smaller tools and weapons were attached to the belt.

The belt was perhaps the most important symbol of a Roman soldier. In some ways it was even more important than armor or weapons. Only Roman soldiers and some civil servants wore decorated belts. The belt was so important to the Roman soldier that it was considered a serious punishment to deprive a soldier of his belt, or even his right to wear his belt. An article about ancient Roman weaponry informs us:

> [The] belt provided identification and identity to a legionnaire. There was no other identifying information anywhere on the standard uniform…the cloak and tunic worn by soldiers was similar to what civilians would wear. The belt identified a soldier as a soldier. The attached silver or bronze pieces would provide whatever identification there might be. Decorations for a unit or individual would be worn on one of the straps.
>
> Juvenal [a Roman poet and satirist of the first century AD] is cited as describing soldiers as "armed and belted men." If a legionnaire was dishonorably discharged, one ancient source (Herodian) says the soldier would be stripped of his belt, thus removing his identity. (Ulvog, 2019)[1]

---

1. Ulvog, J. July 6, 2019. Balteus or cingulum– belt worn by Roman Legionnaires. Pugio– dagger carried by soldiers. Ancient Finances. https://ancientfinances.com/2019/07/06/balteus-or-cingulum-belt-worn-by-roman-legionnaires-puglio-dagger-carried-by-soldiers/

The Warrior's Walk

The late Bible teacher Chuck Missler of Koinonia House wrote:

> It should come as no surprise that Paul begins his list of spiritual armor with "being girded with truth." The real truth: the Word of God.
>
> The Roman belt was 6-8 inches wide; all the body armor and weapons were attached to it. As a soldier's belt gave ease and freedom of movement, so truth gives freedom with self, others, and God.
>
> All was prepared before, not during, the battle! You can't postpone the gaining of combat knowledge to when you "need" it!...
>
> One definition of truth is when the Word and Deed become one. The ultimate truth is the fulfillment of God's promises in His Messiah. God's Word had committed Him to provide what we need in His Son. Jesus was the fulfillment of that commitment.
>
> Jesus saith unto him, I am the Way, the Truth, and the Life: no man cometh unto the Father, but by me. John 14:6
>
> This is the basis of our armor in any spiritual battle. All other elements of our warfare derive from this.
>
> What is our most dangerous source of lies? Ourselves! God desires truth in our inward parts. This is why we are admonished to "take every thought captive." This brings us to a key "life verse":
>
> I beseech you therefore, brethren, by the mercies of God, that ye present your bodies a living sacrifice, holy, acceptable unto God, which is your reasonable service.

> And be not conformed to this world: but be transformed by the renewing of your mind, that you may prove what is that good, and acceptable, and perfect, will of God. (Romans 12:1–2)
>
> Only by renewing our minds-and challenging the lies that drive our society, can we achieve a better destiny than the fate toward which we now stumble. (Missler, 1996)[2]

We've established that the belt was the foundational part of the armor, and also learned that the belt provided the identity and identification of the soldier wearing it. Likewise, truth is foundational to our living victorious lives. Our identity in Christ and His blood with which we are stamped and sealed is our identification.

There are six areas of truth that we must know and understand in order for the belt of truth to be securely buckled:

- Truth about the Godhead
- Truth about Scripture and doctrine
- Truth about who we are
- Truth about who the enemy is
- Truth as pertains to reality
- Truth in the inward parts

Truth about the Godhead:

One of the clearest statements of the deity of Christ anywhere in the Bible is **Colossians 2:8–9**:

> *See to it that no one takes you captive through philosophy and empty deception, according to the tradition of men, according to the elementary principles of the world, rather than according to*

---

2. Missler, C. 1996. The armor of God, the quest for truth. Koinonia House. https://www.khouse.org/articles/1996/67/print/)

Christ. For in Him all the fullness of Deity dwells in bodily form...

This verse states that Jesus is God Incarnate. He embodies all "the fulness" of God. This is corroborated by Colossians 1:19, which says that God was pleased to have all His fullness dwell in Him.

Jesus affirmed that the Godhead is the essence or nature of God when He declared, "I and the Father are One" (John 10:30) and when He told Phillip, "He who has seen me has seen the Father" (John 14:9). The Godhead is not comprised of three gods. God is one.

Truth about Scripture and Doctrine

False teachings abound, even in the Christian community, and some traditions that aren't necessarily bad or wrong are simply traditions of human origin. Jesus dealt with the same problem in His day:

> **Matthew 23:1–4**
> *Then Jesus spoke to the crowds and to His disciples, saying: "The scribes and the Pharisees have seated themselves in the chair of Moses; therefore, all that they tell you, do and observe, but do not do according to their deeds; for they say things and do not do them. They tie up heavy burdens and lay them on men's shoulders, but they themselves are unwilling to move them with so much as a finger.*

While there's some speculation over what the seat of Moses was—for instance, was it an actual seat or was it symbolic—it's clear that the person or teacher in that position would read and teach from the Torah. Jesus instructed people to listen to what was taught from Holy Scripture and to do it, but not to follow the hypocritical lifestyle and deeds of those speaking.

The apostle Paul advised that Scripture be held in the highest regard:

> **2 Timothy 3:16**
> *All Scripture is inspired by God and profitable for teaching, for*

reproof, for correction, for training in righteousness; so that the man of God may be adequate, equipped for every good work.

To understand Scripture and correctly apply it to our lives, we need to put on our "hermeneutical glasses." An article in Christianity Today explains:

> The first is to assume that the Bible, in general, says what it means. That is, the Bible is generally to be interpreted literally, taking the plain meaning of the passage over a more complicated, esoteric interpretation, unless it's obviously meant to be symbolic or a figure of speech.
>
> A second tip is to consider the passage in context. What was the historical context? Who wrote it? Who were they writing to, if anyone? Why? What was the cultural context? What was going on at the time?
>
> Finally, it's essential to interpret the passage within the context of the Bible itself. What verses precede and follow the passage? What is the passage as a whole about? What about the book? Is it referencing a different part of Scripture? (Roat, 2020)[3]

Paul commended the Bereans for being diligent and committed to the written word:

Acts 17:11
Now these were more noble-minded than those in Thessalonica, for they received the word with great eagerness, examining the Scriptures daily to see whether these things were so.

---

3. Roat, A. June 22, 2020. What is hermeneutics? History and methods of biblical interpretation. Christianity Today. https://www.christianity.com/wiki/bible/meaning-origin-history-of-biblical-hermeneutics.html

We must be just as diligent. When we hear or read someone's teachings, it's imperative to search the Scriptures to make sure that it aligns with God's word.

Truth about Who We Are

We are created in God's image (Genesis 1:27)
God created man in His own image, in the image of God He created him; male and female He created them.

We are the children of God (Romans 8:16)
The Spirit Himself testifies with our spirit that we are children of God...

We are forgiven (1 John 1:9)
If we confess our sins, he is faithful and just and will forgive us our sins and purify us from all unrighteousness.

We are saved by God's grace (Ephesians 2:8)
"For by grace you have been saved through faith; and that not of yourselves, it is the gift of God"

We are justified (Romans 5:1)
Therefore, having been justified by faith, we have peace with God through our Lord Jesus Christ.

We are new creatures (2 Corinthians 5:17)
Therefore if anyone is in Christ, he is a new creature; the old things passed away; behold, new things have come.

We are strong in the Lord (Ephesians 6:10)
Finally, be strong in the Lord and in the strength of His might.

When we do not know who we are in God's kingdom, we can be easily blindsided by attacks from the enemy.

The Belt of Truth

Truth about the Enemy:

What is the mission of Satan and those who do his bidding?

- To wage war against those who obey God's commandments and hold to the testimony of Jesus (Rev. 12:17).
- To steal, kill, and destroy (John 10:10).
- To murder and lie (John 8:44).
- To deceive and distort the truth (2 Cor. 11:3, 1 Tim. 4:1).
- To influence the way people behave. To tempt and seduce people into sin.
- To accuse God's children.
- To discourage and keep people from being productive and effective for God.
- To use religion as a yoke of oppression and a substitute for intimacy with Jesus.

We can't effectively fight the battle if we don't know who or what the enemy is and what we are up against. Satan's lies don't usually appear in their bare ugliness; they come in prettily wrapped packages with bright bows and ribbons. Just because something looks good on the surface doesn't mean there isn't anything bad underneath.

Many organizations, groups, and religious or spiritual-sounding movements engage in benevolent and philanthropic activities for individuals and communities. But when you dig deeper you find they also support abortion, sexual deviancy and lasciviousness, or they promote New Age and occult practices, or they contribute money to anti-Christian, anti-family causes.

Consider this; before being identified as such, counterfeit money can be used for good things (feeding the hungry, clothing the naked, helping the poor), but it won't pass inspection at the bank. Likewise, false religions and false teachers can promote morality or do good things in a community, but as far as their ability to point the way to eternal life, they won't pass inspection at the Judgment Bar of Christ.

Truth as pertains to Reality

What's happening in the world around us? One of my maxims is *Truth is the currency of reality*. If we're not living according to truth, we are in a fantasy world. Reality is all we have to work with to make wise and sound decisions. That's being founded on a rock. Anything other than operating in truth is building on shifting sand, and when the rains come and the winds blow, great will be our fall. Here are some examples:

- Voting for a candidate whose promises are different than his actions.
- Basing your decisions on what you read or hear in the mainstream media. Even alternative media needs to be vetted.
- Making important medical and health decisions based on so-called science without doing investigation of your own. (Follow the money. Who benefits most from certain therapies?)
- Believing a religious teaching or doctrine just because it came over the pulpit or from a popular pastor or evangelist. Ensure it aligns with the Word of God.
- Being in denial about an abusive or destructive relationship.
- Being in denial about your spiritual condition.
- Being blind to your own faults.

Truth in the Inward Parts

Jeremiah 17:9
The prophet Jeremiah tells us the problem: "The heart is more deceitful than all else, And is desperately sick; Who can understand it?

Psalm 51:6
But this is what God requires; King David writes: "Behold, You desire truth in the inward parts, And in the hidden part You will make me to know wisdom."

This psalm of David is one of his most vulnerable and heartfelt prayers after his sin with Bathsheba was revealed by the Prophet Nathan. He was laid bare and truly exposed. The truth about his affair was out and could not be hidden any longer.

Have you ever been in that place where the gig was up and everyone knew about your failure, shortcoming, or sin? That is where David was. He knew he had sinned greatly against the Lord, and it hit him like a ton of bricks—not just because he had been exposed outwardly, but it hurt him deep in his soul because he realized how much he had grieved God.

We need to make a daily assessment of ourselves. Have we been honest with God? He already knows everything about us. What He desires is authenticity and repentance. We need to lay ourselves bare before Him. He already knows if we're angry or hurt or irritated or stubborn. So just come clean!

It's also important to be honest with *ourselves*. That means not making excuses for bad behavior or wrong-doing. How can we expect to improve our relationships, cease destructive habits, or make positive improvements in our lives if we don't examine ourselves with honest assessment?

Tying this all together, what we are doing when we put on the belt of truth is committing ourselves to embracing truth, acting in truth, and being a vessel of truth every day.

This lighthearted example illustrates how imperative it is to use discernment in all our endeavors. We've probably all been approached by slick salespeople trying to convince us to buy their dubious products. My daughter and I were at a mall in Denver when a pushy guy at a beauty care kiosk pulled me over, had me sit down, and started putting all kinds of creams and serums on half my face. He peered intently at me, pleased with himself, and declared that one side of my face now looked ten years younger as a result of his skincare products.

After 15-minutes of slathering me up and giving me a sales pitch, he took a picture to show me the difference between the left and right sides of my face. Emperor's new clothes. One side looked dry and wrinkled, the other side looked greasy and wrinkled; fig vs. prune.

The picture was awful. I shook my head in disbelief and said, "Oh my gosh, I look like my mother!"

"Honey," he replied, "Everyone looks like their mother."

"My mother is dead," I replied, imagining her wrinkled corpse. "And she was old when she died and I look just like her."

Uncomfortable laughter escaped the man's lips. Unconvinced about the effectiveness of his "miracle creams," I quickly got up from the chair and left without buying anything.

Flattery might work at times when trying to convince someone they're something that in reality they are not, but we need to be careful to not let ourselves be swept away in the moment when emotions are high and we want to believe that something is true.

So what should we believe? Lies wrapped in "truth's clothing" or "the naked truth?" That's really the choice before us. Who and what are we going to believe?

We must have the belt of truth securely buckled every minute of the day to avoid being deceived. The reason Satan's lies are so effective is because they are wrapped in truth's clothing; but God has given us the naked truth right in His written Word. If we are to defend ourselves against the devil's falsehoods, we must be armed with God's truth. Only then can we stand firm.

5
The Breastplate of Righteousness

He put on righteousness like a breastplate...
Isaiah 59:17

What comes to my mind when thinking about the breastplate of righteousness is the story of young David preparing to go up against Goliath. I see a great correlation to the breastplate of righteousness and the armor of God as a whole.

The Philistines challenged Israel to a battle for 40 days. Forty days is significant in Scripture because it typically signifies a time of testing or trial. Think of Moses going up Mount Sinai or Jesus fasting in the wilderness. That time period is followed by deliverance or by chastisement of some kind. This particular battle was more than just one of the common conflicts of the day. This event was God-ordained and had a divine purpose.

David's father, Jesse, sends his three oldest sons to represent his family in the war, and after 40 days of them being gone, he begins to worry about their welfare. He tells David to check up on them and bring provisions. Israel didn't have a professional military back then. Each fighting man was responsible to supply his own weaponry and food. David arrives to check on his brothers just as Goliath comes out to shout his challenge and insults to the Israelites. To his surprise, no one steps forward or volunteers!

He overhears a soldier say that whoever defeats the Philistine champion will not only get to marry the king's daughter, but his whole family will be exempt from paying taxes and contributing labor and resources to the kingdom from that time forward. Amazed, David asks, "Who is this uncircumcised Philistine that defies the army of the Living God?"

When David uses the expression "The Living God," it meant more to the ancient Israelites than what we may think. Today we tend to think of it as meaning the opposite of atheism—that unbelievers will see and know that there is a God in Israel. However, the Hebrew people were not monotheists. They, and the nations around them, believed in many gods and that these gods had territorial dominion.

So, when nations went to war, it was much more than whose army was bigger and stronger. Wars in ancient times signified to the people whose gods were stronger and more powerful. Israel was the laughingstock of the ancient world because they only had one God while the other nations served many gods.

The expression David uses is *Elohim Chayim*, the Living God—meaning God of Life, the Active God who is involved in our everyday comings and goings. David is concerned most of all about Yahweh's reputation. When it becomes clear that David was actually considering going up against the heathen giant, someone runs and tells King Saul. This account is recorded in **1 Samuel 17:31–51 (CJB)**:

> *David's words were overheard and told to Saul, who summoned him. David said to Saul, "No one should lose heart because of him; your servant will go and fight this Philistine." Saul said to David, "You can't go to fight this Philistine — you're just a boy, and he has been a warrior from his youth!"*
>
> *David answered Saul, "Your servant used to guard his father's sheep. When a lion or a bear would come and grab a lamb from*

the flock, I would go after it, hit it, and snatch the lamb from its mouth; and if it turned on me, I would catch it by the jaw, smack it and kill it.

Your servant has defeated both lions and bears, and this uncircumcised Philistine will be like one of them, because he has challenged the armies of the living God." Then David said, "Adonai, who rescued me from the paw of the lion and from the paw of the bear, will rescue me from the paw of this Philistine!" Saul said to David, "Go; may Adonai be with you."

Saul dressed David in his own armor — he put a bronze helmet on his head and gave him armor plate to wear. David buckled his sword on his armor and tried to walk, but he wasn't used to such equipment. David said to Saul, "I can't move wearing these things, because I'm not used to them." So David took them off.

Then he took his stick in his hand and picked five smooth stones from the riverbed, putting them in his shepherd's bag, in his pouch. Then, with his sling in his hand, he approached the Philistine.

The Philistine, with his shield-bearer ahead of him, came nearer and nearer to David. The Philistine looked David up and down and had nothing but scorn for what he saw — a boy with ruddy cheeks, red hair and good looks. The Philistine said to David, "Am I a dog? Is that why you're coming at me with sticks?" — and Goliath cursed David by his god.

Then the Philistine said to David, "Come here to me, so I can give your flesh to the birds in the air and the wild animals."

David answered the Philistine, "You're coming at me with a sword, a spear and a javelin. But I'm coming at you in the name of Adonai-Tzva'ot, the God of the armies of Isra'el, whom you have challenged.

Today Adonai will hand you over to me. I will attack you, lop your head off, and give the carcasses of the army of the Philistines to the birds in the air and the animals in the land. Then all the land will know that there is a God in Isra'el, and everyone assembled here will know that Adonai does not save by sword or spear. For this is Adonai's battle, and he will hand you over to us."

When Goliath got up, approached and came close to meet David, David hurried and ran toward the army to meet the Philistine. David put his hand in his bag, took out a stone, and hurled it with his sling. It struck the Philistine in his forehead and buried itself in his forehead, so that he fell face down on the ground.

Thus David defeated Goliath with a sling and a stone, striking the Philistine and killing him; but David had no sword in his hand. Then David ran and stood over the Philistine, took his sword, drew it out of its sheath, and finished killing him, cutting off his head with it. When the Philistines saw that their hero was dead, they fled.

King Saul tried to discourage David by warning he was only a boy and Goliath a seasoned warrior from his youth. That's like us being discouraged when we feel defeated and the enemy taunts us; "Humans are weak and no match against demons and fallen angels. We are powerful and have been causing destruction for thousands of years. You cannot prevail against us!"

David recounts to the king that he was rescued from the lion and bear, and states with confidence that God will rescue him from the giant Philistine. Likewise, we can say, "Adonai, who rescued me from sin and death, will rescue me from the hand of Satan." We will prevail because Jesus already won the victory at Calvary.

David attempts to put on Saul's armor, but it's so heavy and cumbersome he can't fight in it. He hadn't yet "tested it" before going to battle. Neither can we do battle with worldly weapons or secular techniques. Paul wrote:

The Breastplate of Righteousness

2 Corinthians 10:3–4
For although we do live in the world, we do not wage war in a worldly way; because the weapons we use to wage war are not worldly.

David takes a stone in his hand. We take the Living Stone, Jesus Christ, in ours. With the power of the sling, David embeds the stone into Goliath's forehead, causing him to fall facedown to the earth. With the power of the blood of Messiah, our enemy is defeated, and all who follow Satan will fall facedown before the King of Glory and confess that Jesus is LORD. David stands over Goliath and finishes him off with the sword, and the Philistine army flees. And we will defeat the demonic realm with the sword of the Spirit, which is the word of God. We're told to resist the devil and he will flee.

We don't need techniques, gimmicks, or small-g-gods. One God and His blood shed for us is sufficient!

Ephesians 6:14
Stand therefore, having fastened on the belt of truth, and having put on the breastplate of righteousness...

We see that we must put on truth before we can put on righteousness. Why? Because if there isn't a foundation of truth, man will attempt to put on his own righteousness and justify himself by his own good works. Once we are grounded in truth, we are then ready to be clothed with the righteousness of our Messiah.

In the natural, a soldier's breastplate protects vital organs: the heart, lungs, intestines, and so forth. Injury to any one of these could result in death. The heart keeps the blood circulating. Lungs oxygenate the blood. The intestines digest food by taking nutrients out of what we eat and dispersing them to the cells, and then eliminating waste material. Truly, the life is in the blood (Leviticus 17:11).

The heart propels blood through our vessels with every beat. Do our hearts beat for the Almighty? Our lungs keep our blood infused with life-sustaining oxygen. Is God the very "air we breathe?"

Genesis 2:7
Then the Lord God formed the man of dust from the ground and breathed into his nostrils the breath of life, and the man became a living creature.

Job 33:4
The Spirit of God has made me, and the breath of the Almighty gives me life.

Our digestive system is a critical part of good health. It's important to eat nutritious foods for our physical health, and it's important that our spiritual diet is healthy. Jesus is the Bread of Life and Living Water. He instructs us to partake of the bread representing His body that was broken for us, and to drink the wine representing His blood that was shed for us.

Just as we have to be careful about what we take into our bodies physically, we need to be careful about what we take into our bodies and minds spiritually. Do we guard our eyes and ears in regard to what we see and listen to? Paul instructs:

Philippians 4:8
Whatever is true, whatever is honorable, whatever is right, whatever is pure, whatever is lovely, whatever is commendable, if there is any excellence and if anything worthy of praise, think about these things.

It's so easy to get caught up in the bad news of the day and to be overwhelmed by it. For our own well-being and peace of mind we have to pursue righteousness and not be overcome by evil, but to overcome evil with good.

A spiritual breastplate guards and protects the most vital parts of our soul. The armor doesn't keep us from being attacked and it doesn't keep us from experiencing pushback. However, it does keep us from fatal blows. By the power of God we can arise and recover. This reminds me of Kevlar, bulletproof clothing: The Dupont website describes it:

The Breastplate of Righteousness

Kevlar fibers are so tightly spun that it is nearly impossible to separate them. When a bullet or other high-velocity projectile hits Kevlar, the fibers essentially catch the projectile while absorbing and dissipating its energy. (Dupont, n.d.)[1]

If you're wearing Kevlar and get struck by a bullet, it may leave a painful bruise from the impact, but it won't kill you.

The breastplate is first mentioned in **Isaiah 59:15-17**:

> *Truth is lacking, he who leaves evil becomes a target.*
> *Adonai saw it, and it displeased him that there was no justice. He saw that there was no one, was amazed that no one interceded.*
>
> *Therefore his own arm brought him salvation,*
> *and his own righteousness sustained him.*
>
> *He put on righteousness as his breastplate, salvation as a helmet on his head.*

The breastplate is mentioned again in **1 Thessalonians 5:8**, *"But since we belong to the day, let us be sober, having put on the breastplate of faith and love..."* This time we're encouraged to put on faith and love as a breastplate.

When Paul says to "put on the new man" or "put on the armor of God," he uses the Greek word *enduo*, which literally means to "sink into." So when we put on the armor or each individual piece, we aren't just adorning ourselves outwardly—we are sinking into or immersing ourselves in the corresponding characteristics. In other words, it's the way we live everyday life; putting on faith and love and clothing ourselves with our Lord's righteousness.

Each day we have to decide if we're going to live according to the ways of the world or if we will walk in our Savior's footsteps.

---

1. "What is Kevlar ®?," Dupont, https://www.dupont.com/what-is-kevlar.html

The *Moody Bible Commentary*, quoted in Christianity.com says:

> Although prayer is important for the process [of putting on the armor] believers do not 'pray' the armor onto themselves. Putting on the armor has to do with our moral choices—our lifestyle—that provide protection against the temptations of the world and the devil. (Siler, 2022).[2]

We don't want to open any doors to the demonic through willful sin. But ultimately, while we do our best to walk in His ways and make godly choices, we need to remember it's not our own efforts that save us. The enemy will try to beat us down by saying we're not good enough or worthy enough, but we can say, "Get lost, Satan; I am covered by the blood of the Lamb and I am clothed in HIS righteousness."

Look again at **Ephesians 6:14** where Paul writes; *"Stand firm therefore, having belted your waist with truth, and having put on the breastplate of righteousness..."* Because we *have* put on the breastplate of righteousness (and the other pieces of armor), we can stand firm against the attacks of the evil one.

How is that accomplished? How do we fight against a realm we can't see when physical and spiritual attacks come? We "sink into" the righteousness of Christ and the other armor God has given us. We pray, and we pray with confidence. We pray from a position of victory by remembering we're united with our Messiah Jesus. We're one with Him; and since He is victorious, we can be too. Prayer is vital to putting on and securing the breastplate:

Ephesians 6:18
As you pray at all times, with all kinds of prayers and requests, in the Spirit, vigilantly and persistently, for all God's people.

---

2. Siler, Josie. "What Is the Breastplate of Righteousness in the Armor of God?" Christianity.Com. September 22, 2022. https://www.christianity.com/wiki/christian-terms/what-is-the-breastplate-of-righteousness.html.

The Breastplate of Righteousness

I love this explanation from GotQuestions.org:

> As we wear Christ's breastplate of righteousness, we begin to develop a purity of heart that translates into actions. Wearing this breastplate creates a lifestyle of putting into practice what we believe in our hearts. As our lives become conformed to the image of Christ (Romans 8:29), our choices become more righteous, and these godly choices also protect us from further temptation and deception (Proverbs 8:20; Psalm 23:3).[3]

What is it like to have on the armor? Imagine a chilly winter's night where you have a fire blazing in the fireplace, and you wrap yourself in a soft, fuzzy blanket, and sink into your favorite overstuffed rocking recliner with a cup of hot chocolate or a latte in your hand (you can spike it if you want). You are totally ensconced from the storm outside. You know you are protected from the elements. That's what it's like to have on the full armor of God. It's not a big, clunky, heavy metal suit that's subject to rust and decay. Think of *mithril* in Lord of the Rings. The character Gandalf describes it like this:

> Mithril! All folk desired it. It could be beaten like copper, and polished like glass; and the Dwarves could make of it a metal, light and yet harder than tempered steel. Its beauty was like to that of common silver, but the beauty of mithril did not tarnish or grow dim. (Gateway, "Mithril - Tolkien Gateway.")[4]

The armor of God is beautiful, functional, and enduring. It's not like King Saul's armor on David, and it's not a burden. Jesus said:

---

[3]. "What is the Breastplate of Righteousness?" Got Questions Ministries, accessed February 20, 2024, https://www.gotquestions.org/breastplate-of-righteousness.html
[4]. Tolkien Gateway, "Mithril - Tolkien Gateway," Tolkien Gateway, January 13, 2023, https://tolkiengateway.net/wiki/Mithril.

Matt. 11:28–29
Come to me, all of you who are struggling and burdened, and I will give you rest. Take my yoke upon you and learn from me, because I am gentle and humble in heart, and you will find rest for your souls. For my yoke is easy, and my burden is light."

Likewise, the armor of God is light and not meant to be burdensome. Wearing it will not keep us out of the battle, but it will provide a solid defense from attack, and the tools to engage effectively and successfully.

6

Shoes of the Gospel of Peace

*How beautiful on the mountains
are the feet of the messenger who brings good news,
the good news of peace and salvation,
the news that the God of Israel reigns!
Isaiah 52:7*

A vital part of donning the armor is "having shod your feet with the preparation of the gospel of peace" (Eph. 6:15). What do these shoes represent and how are they to be worn? The key word in this verse—depending on which Bible translation you use—is "preparation" or "readiness," which comes from the Greek word *hetoimasia* (pronounced heh-toy-ma-SEE-ah). It means the act of preparing:

> To make ready, prepare, to make the necessary preparations, get everything ready.
>
> Metaphorically, it's drawn from the Middle Eastern custom of sending persons ahead of kings on their journeys persons to level the roads and make them passable.

To prepare the minds of men to give the Messiah a fit reception and secure his blessings (BibleStudyTools, n.d.).[1]

John the Immerser's specific role and calling was to be the voice in the wilderness prophesied by Isaiah. The gospel of **John 1:19, 23**:

> *Now this is the testimony of John, when the Jews sent priests and Levites from Jerusalem to ask him, "Who are you?"*
> *He said: "I am 'The voice of one crying in the wilderness: "Make straight the way of the Lord,"' as the prophet Isaiah said."*

And from **Isaiah 40:3–5**:

> *The voice of one crying in the wilderness:*
> *"Prepare the way of the Lord; Make straight in the desert A highway for our God.*
> *Every valley shall be exalted And every mountain and hill brought low;*
> *The crooked places shall be made straight And the rough places smooth;*
> *The glory of the Lord shall be revealed, And all flesh shall see it together;*
> *For the mouth of the Lord has spoken."*

What does it mean for us to make His paths straight and level the road, to make it passable? Rather than being a stumbling block for others, it's essential to be winsome as we tell people about Jesus. In other words, if any offense is taken, let it be because of the message and not because of a confrontational delivery.

---

1. "Hetoimazo Meaning - Greek Lexicon: New Testament (NAS)." Bible Study Tools. Accessed February 21, 2024. https://www.biblestudytools.com/lexicons/greek/nas/hetoimazo.html.

Philippians 4:5, CBJ
Let everyone see how reasonable and gentle you are. The Lord is near.

Colossians 3:12
Therefore, as God's chosen people, holy and dearly loved, clothe yourselves with compassion, kindness, humility, gentleness and patience.

Galatians 6:10
Therefore, as we have opportunity, let us do good to all people, especially to those who belong to the family of believers.

Proverbs 16:24
Gracious words are a honeycomb, sweet to the soul and healing to the bones.

Proverbs 15:1
A gentle answer turns away wrath, but a harsh word stirs up anger.

1 Peter 3:15, AMP
But in your hearts set Christ apart as Lord [as holy, acknowledging Him, giving Him first place in your lives. Always be ready to give a [logical] defense to anyone who asks you to account for the hope and confident assurance that is within you, yet [do it] with gentleness and respect.

And see to it that your conscience is entirely clear, so that every time you are slandered or falsely accused, those who attack or disparage your good behavior in Christ will be shamed [by their own words].

Colossians 4:5–6, NASB
Conduct yourselves with wisdom toward outsiders, making the most of the opportunity. Your speech must always be with

grace, as though seasoned with salt, so that you will know how you should respond to each person.

Zechariah 7:9–10
This is what the Lord Almighty said: 'Administer true justice; show mercy and compassion to one another. Do not oppress the widow or the fatherless, the foreigner or the poor. Do not plot evil against each other.'

All these words are torah to us; *torah*, meaning God's loving instruction to show us how we are to walk according to His will. When we have our feet shod with the preparation of the gospel of peace, we are letting the light of Jesus shine through us, as illustrated by this story:

> On a cold day in December, a little boy, about 10 years old was standing before a shoe store on the roadway, barefoot, peering through the window, and shivering with cold. A lady approached the boy and said, "My little fellow, why are you looking so earnestly in that window?"
>
> "I was asking God to give me a pair of shoes," was the boy's reply. The lady took him by the hand and went into the store and asked the clerk to get half a dozen pairs of socks for the boy. She then asked if he could give her a basin of water and a towel. He quickly brought them to her. She took the little fellow to the back part of the store and, removing her gloves, knelt down, washed his little feet, and dried them with a towel.
>
> By this time the clerk had returned with the socks. Placing a pair upon the boy's feet, she purchased him a pair of shoes. She tied up the remaining pairs of socks and gave them to him. She patted him on the head and said, "No doubt, my little fellow, you feel more comfortable now?"
>
> As she turned to go, the astonished lad caught her by

the hand, and looking up in her face, with tears his eyes, answered the question with these words: "Are you God's wife?" (Traditional, n.d.).[2]

We must always be prepared to demonstrate the love of God, not only in word, but in deed.

It's interesting that there are only two pieces of armor that can be given away and yet automatically replenished: the Belt of Truth and the Shoes of the Gospel. We cannot give the helmet of salvation to another; it's bestowed on them by God. We cannot give away the breastplate of righteousness, because Jesus imputes His righteousness to the individual believer. We cannot give the shield of faith to anyone, because faith is something that must be developed in oneself. The sword of the Spirit belongs to the Holy Spirit, which indwells a person upon salvation.

However, the belt of truth and the shoes of the gospel can be disseminated to others. Whether they take hold of truth or the message of redemption is up to them, but if we are wearing our armor appropriately, we'll be purveyors of truth and the gospel of Christ wherever we go. Always be prepared to share the good news about Jesus. Give the gospel away!

It's said that as the Indian social activist Mahatma Gandhi stepped aboard a train one day, one of his shoes slipped off and landed on the track. The train was moving, making it impossible for him to retrieve it. Gandhi took his other shoe and threw it onto the track, landing it near his other shoe. A fellow passenger was perplexed and asked him why he did that. Gandhi smiled and replied, "The poor man who finds the shoes lying on the track will now have a pair he can use."[3]

You cannot go many places expeditiously with only one shoe on, nor will you win any races (unless all the contestants are running with one shoeless foot). It takes a pair of good shoes to be ready for a journey or a battle.

Why "shoes" as part of the armor? In any daily activity, especially

---

2. Traditional. "Are You God' [sic] Wife?" Logos Sermons, n.d.. Accessed February 22, 2024. https://sermons.logos.com/sermons/84052-are-you-god'-wife.
3. Multiple online sources for this anecdote about Ghandi.

outdoors, shoes provide protection, defense, and traction. *Barnes' Notes on the Whole Bible* explains;

> And your feet shod - There is undoubtedly an allusion here to what was worn by the ancient soldier to guard his feet. The Greek is, literally, "having under-bound the feet;" that is, having bound on the shoes, or sandals, or whatever was worn by the ancient soldier. The protection of the feet and ankles consisted of two parts:
>
> (1) The sandals, or shoes, which were probably made so as to cover the foot, and which often were fitted with nails, or armed with spikes, to make the hold firm in the ground: or,
>
> (2) With "greaves" that were fitted to the legs, and designed to defend them from any danger. These "greaves," or boots [what we might call "shin guards"] were made of brass, and were in almost universal use among the Greeks and Romans.
>
> With the preparation - Prepared with the gospel of peace. The sense is, that the Christian soldier is to be prepared with the gospel of peace to meet attacks similar to those against which the ancient soldier designed to guard himself by the sandals or greaves which he wore. It is difficult to determine the exact meaning; and perhaps all expositors have erred in endeavoring to explain the reference of these parts of armor by some particular thing in the gospel.
>
> The apostle figured to himself a soldier, clad in the usual manner. Christians were to resemble him. One part of his dress or preparation consisted in the covering and defense of the foot. It was to preserve the foot from danger, and to secure the facility of his march, and perhaps to make

Shoes of the Gospel of Peace

him firm in battle (Barnes, n.d.).[4]

We must have the right shoes for the right occasion. We wouldn't wear flip flops to a formal dinner or to go hiking in the woods. This reminds me of a story about two men and a bear:

> Two friends were walking through the woods when they attracted the attention of a vicious-looking bear. The bear noticed them and started to lumber toward them. The first man immediately opened his backpack, pulled out a pair of sneakers and started putting them on. The second man looked at him and said: "You're crazy! You'll never be able to outrun that bear!"
>
> "Oh, I know that. Bears are much faster than humans. I have no hope of ever being able to outrun a bear."
>
> "If you know that, why are you changing shoes?" his friend asked.
>
> "Well, the way I figure it," the first man replied. "I don't have to outrun the bear. I only need to outrun you."

Humans cannot outrun bears, and we can't outrun demons or whatever other entities that may come upon the earth. We're not looking for trouble, but when it comes, we have to stand firm and face the opposition.

Remember, Roman infantrymen wore tough sandals that were studded with thick, sharp nails on the bottoms to increase their traction. The bottom of our shoes are fitted with the nails that pierced our Savior's hands and feet. The time is soon upon us—and in fact is already here—when we have to dig in our heels and resist enemy forces.

From Dr. Thomas Constable's commentary on Ephesians;

---

4. Barnes, Albert. "Commentary on Ephesians 6:15". "Barnes' Notes on the Whole Bible". https://www.studylight.org/commentary

The gospel that has brought peace to the Christian enables him or her to stand firmly against temptation. Likewise, the gospel is what enables us to move forward against our enemies. The preparation of the gospel of peace probably refers to the gospel the Christian soldier has believed that enables him to stand his ground when attacked.

We must be so familiar with the gospel that we can share it with others. That grip on the gospel will enable us to hold our ground and even advance when tempted. The gospel in view is the whole Christian message viewed as good news, not just how to become a Christian (Constable, 2012).[5]

I found a testimony that fits in so well with shoes. The little things are the big things. Here's one man's story:

> When I got sober my sponsor told me that I had to be willing to change everything about my life—everything. So, I wore blue jeans and switched to slacks. I wore western shirts and switched to T-shirts. But the one thing I just couldn't give up was my cowboy boots.
>
> I went to my sponsor and said, "Surely, I won't get drunk over a silly pair of cowboy boots. I'm willing to change a lot of things, and if needed I could even give up those boots, but it seems so silly."
>
> My sponsor said, "I don't know how silly it is, or if you'll get drunk over those cowboy boots, but I can tell that you are not 'entirely' willing to change."

---

5. Constable, Thomas. Dr. "Commentary on Ephesians 6:15". "Dr. Constable's Expository Notes". https://www.studylight.org/commentaries/eng/dcc/ephesians-6.html

"Okay, okay," I said. "I'll prove it to you. I'll give up the boots for 30 days just to demonstrate my willingness to God."

So, I bought a pair of tennis shoes, and after 30 days of not wearing my cowboy boots, wearing tennis shoes instead, the strangest thing happened—my feet stopped hurting.

That's how it was getting sober and giving up the high life. I never stopped to think that the boots were causing my feet to hurt, or the booze was causing my life to hurt. I got willing to give up the stuff, one day at a time, for 30 days, then 60 days, then 90 days … and my life stopped hurting.

And every day I do something different, some change in some small way. Maybe I just put my socks on different or drive to work a new way. Every day, I try to do Little Things in a Big Way so that when Big Things happen, I can handle them in a Little Way (Unknown, 2020).[6]

Are we willing to take off our spiritual cowboy boots or cozy slippers and suit up for battle? It takes being willing to do God's will instead of our own. To do this we have to be willing to make sacrifices and give up our comforts. Jesus didn't want to suffer. He wept and prayed in the garden on the night of His arrest, and yet was willing to endure the cross for the joy set before Him:

> **Luke 22:42**
> *"Father, if you are willing, take this cup away from me; still, let not my will but yours be done."*

---

6. Unknown, "New Pair of Shoes, a," Inspirational Stories, Quotes & Poems, February 3, 2020, https://www.inspirationalstories.com/new-pair-of-shoes-a/

Hebrews 12:1–3
Therefore, since we also have such a great cloud of witnesses surrounding us, let's rid ourselves of every obstacle and the sin which so easily entangles us, and let's run with endurance the race that is set before us, looking only at Jesus, the originator and perfecter of the faith, who for the joy set before Him endured the cross, despising the shame, and has sat down at the right hand of the throne of God. For consider Him who has endured such hostility by sinners against Himself, so that you will not grow weary and lose heart.

Jesus understood that a heavenly kingdom was awaiting Him—the one that all the faithful have looked forward to down through the ages:

Hebrews 11:13–16
All these people died still believing what God had promised them. They did not receive what was promised, but they saw it all from a distance and welcomed it. They agreed that they were foreigners and nomads here on earth. Obviously people who say such things are looking forward to a country they can call their own. If they had longed for the country they came from, they could have gone back. But they were looking for a better place, a heavenly homeland. That is why God is not ashamed to be called their God, for he has prepared a city for them.

As described in the Revelation 21:4, there is coming a time when there will be "no more death or sorrow or crying or pain." That is the joy set before all whose faith is placed in Yeshua the Messiah, that we will be with God, and He will be with us, together forever, in the New Jerusalem—that heavenly city coming down to a renewed earth.

Keeping our feet shod with the shoes of the gospel of peace offers protection and traction to we who bring good tidings to everyone around us. These tidings of good will are not conveyed by words alone, but are demonstrated by our acts of service and kindness. Christian artist and writer Leanne Frieberg wrote this poignant poem of the shoes we wear, shared with permission:

Shoes of the Gospel of Peace

The Shoes

My alarm went off
It was Sunday again.
I was sleepy and tired
My one day to sleep in.
But the guilt I would feel
The rest of the day
Would have been too much
So I'd go, and I'd pray.
I showered and shaved
I adjusted my tie.
I got there and sat
In a pew just in time.

Bowing my head in prayer
As I closed my eyes.
I saw the shoe of the man next to me
Touching mine, and I sighed.
With plenty of room on either side
I thought, "Why must our soles touch?"
It bothered me, his shoe touching mine
But it didn't bother him much.

A prayer began: "Our Father"...
I thought, "This man with the shoes
has no pride. They're dusty, worn, and scratched;
Even worse, there are holes on the side!"

"Thank You for blessings," the prayer went on.
The shoe man said a quiet "Amen."
I tried to focus on the prayer
But my thoughts were on his shoes again.
Aren't we supposed to look our best
When walking through that door?
"Well, this certainly isn't it," I thought,

The Warrior's Walk

Glancing toward the floor.
Then the prayer was ended
And the songs and praises rang.
The shoe man was certainly loud
Sounding proud as he sang.
His voice lifted the rafters
His hands were raised up high.
The Lord could surely hear
The shoe man's voice from the sky.

It was time for the offering
And what I threw in was steep.
I watched as the shoe man reached
Into his pockets deep.
I saw what was pulled out
What the shoe man put in.
Then I heard a soft "clink"
as when silver resounds on tin.
The sermon really bored me
To tears, and that's no lie.
It seemed the same for the shoe man
For tears fell from his eyes.

At the end of the service
As is the custom here
We must greet new visitors
And show them all good cheer.
But I felt moved somehow
to meet the man who rose to stand,
So after the closing prayer
I reached over and shook his hand.

He was old and his skin was dark
And his hair was truly a mess
But I thanked him for coming
For being our unknown guest.

Shoes of the Gospel of Peace

He said, "My name is Charlie,
I'm glad to meet you, my friend."
Though there were tears in his eyes
He had a large, and friendly grin.
"Let me explain," he said
Wiping tears from his eyes.

"I've been coming here for months
And you're the first one to say 'Hi.'
I know that my appearance
Is not like all the rest
But I really do try
To always look my best.
I always clean and polish my shoes
Before my very long walk.
But by the time I get here
They're dirty and dusty, like chalk."

My heart filled with pain
and I swallowed to hold back tears,
As he continued to apologize
For daring to sit so near.
He said, "When I get here
I know I must look a sight.
But I thought if I could touch you
Then our souls just might unite."

I was silent for a moment
Knowing whatever was said
Would pale in comparison.
I spoke from my heart, not my head.
"Oh, you've touched me," I said,
"And taught me, in great part;
That the best of any man
Is what is found within his heart."
The rest, I thought,

This shoe man will never ever know.
Like just how thankful I really am
That his dirty shoe touched my soul.[7]

May we always be ready to go ahead of our King and make His paths straight.

Romans 10:15
How beautiful are the feet of them that preach the gospel of peace and bring glad tidings of good things!

---

7. Freiberg, Leanne. The Shoes. Used with permission. It's on several websites, but a beautiful video of the poem can be found here: https://www.youtube.com/watch?v=YKbOxKjuDnc

7

The Helmet of Salvation

*This helmet, I suppose, Was meant to ward off blows.
It's very hot, And weighs a lot, As many a guardsman knows,
So off that helmet goes...*[1]

In Gilbert & Sullivan's operetta *Princess Ida*, King Gama's son Arac—just before the climactic battle—declares he's going to remove his armor on the grounds that it's too uncomfortable. The lyrics to the aria he sings continues his lament about wearing armor to battle:

> This tight-fitting cuirass
> Is but a useless mass
> It's made of steel
> And weighs a deal
> This tight-fitting cuirass
> So off goes that cuirass.[2]

---

1. W.S. Gilbert and Arthur Sullivan, "Gilbert and Sullivan – This Helmet, I Suppose Lyrics," azlyrics.biz, accessed February 22, 2024, https://azlyrics.biz/g/gilbert-and-sullivan-lyrics/gilbert-and-sullivan-this-helmet-i-suppose-lyrics/.
2 ibid.

The character goes on to disdain the various pieces of armor as he removes them just before heading to the battlefront.

I've never been dressed in battle gear, but I know what it's like to wear a helmet. There was a time in my life when my only transportation was a motorcycle. For about a year we didn't have a car, so I would take the motorcycle to run errands and do grocery shopping. I'd hang bags of groceries over the handlebars and strap a case of diapers behind me on the seat.

I always wore a helmet, even before it was a state law. When it was 110 degrees or more in the Las Vegas summer, that helmet became hot! My head would get all sweaty and it was uncomfortable to wear, but I knew it would save my life if I spilled the bike.

Most of us, at least those of us with common sense, take precautions to protect ourselves, whether it's wearing a motorcycle helmet or a seatbelt, or if we're playing sports we don the proper protective equipment. But what is the proper equipment needed to face life in the natural and spiritual dimensions?

We are in a war with the demonic realm, like it or not, acknowledge it or not. Most people wish life would be a picnic, but every person on earth will face sorrow, hardship, and suffering at some point in their lives. Yet despite this truth, many—even believers with an understanding of the devil and his devices—mentally and spiritually dress as if they are taking excursions to the zoo. Instead of suiting up in the armor of God, they don tank-tops, shorts, and flip-flops without giving their spiritual apparel a second thought. Rather than being alert and battle-ready, they stroll along from day to day, spiritually underdressed with no regard to the warning given by the apostle Peter:

1 Peter 5:8 (CJB)
Stay sober, stay alert! Your enemy, the Adversary, stalks about like a roaring lion looking for someone to devour.

How do we put on the helmet of salvation? Using Isaiah 59 as context, the apostle Paul adapts the armor of the "divine warrior" to the spiritual armor that believers must wear (Isa. 59:17, Eph. 6:13–17). How does one "wear salvation as a helmet?"

The Helmet of Salvation

First, it's necessary to know what this helmet is. The righteousness of God and the salvation of His people are often found together in the book of Isaiah. To fulfill and keep the promises made to Israel, He acts to rescue them from their enemies, including their sin, which is the ultimate enemy because it causes separation from God.

This firm promise of God—to redeem us from the eternal consequences of sin—is the foundation of the hope we have in Him as we go through the challenges and difficulties of life. The helmet we wear as followers of our Messiah Yeshua is described by Paul as "the helmet of the hope of salvation" (1 Thess. 5:8).

The hope of salvation doesn't mean we are anxiously hoping we're saved but are unsure if salvation will stick! That kind of hope, that kind of helmet, is not going to hold up in battle. It would be like wearing a knit cap rather than a hard hat at a high risk construction site where falling debris could prove fatal.

When Scripture speaks of hope, it isn't some nebulous wish that everything will turn out okay. The hope of salvation is the firm expectation that God will deliver you from the second death and you will spend eternity in His presence. We have the assurance of salvation, provided we are putting our complete trust in Jesus' work alone on the cross as being sufficient to redeem us.

> **1 Peter 3:15**
> *But sanctify Christ as Lord in your hearts, always being ready to make a defense to everyone who asks you to give an account for the hope that is in you, but with gentleness and respect…*

No one can be "good enough" to merit eternal life by their own righteousness. Not only is it impossible, it negates Christ's work on the cross. If you had to depend on your own goodness, how could you ever know if you've done enough to merit God's favor?

If you are relying on your own works to give you that extra boost to get you into heaven, you can never really be sure where you will end up or if you were righteous enough for God's holy standard of perfection. The only one who can reconcile us to God is Yeshua Hamashiach, Jesus the Messiah. Only God Himself could pay the penalty for our sins, and thus we are in need of salvation.

What exactly is salvation? Salvation is also referred to as "deliverance" and "redemption," terms that are slightly nuanced, but signify "being saved." In its simplest form, salvation means to be saved or delivered from something. Biblically speaking, it means being delivered *from* the kingdom of darkness where sin results in an eternal death penalty. When we receive salvation, we are delivered *into* the Kingdom of God, which results in living eternally in God's presence and being heirs of everything He has to offer us as His adopted sons and daughters.

Sometimes called *The Romans Road*, this is what the New Testament says about sin and salvation:

Romans 3:23
For all have sinned, and fall short of the glory of God.

Romans 6:23a
For the wages of sin is death.

Romans 6:23b
But the gracious gift of God is eternal life in Christ Jesus our Lord.

Romans 5:8–11
But God demonstrates His own love toward us, in that while we were still sinners, Christ died for us. Much more then, having now been justified by His blood, we shall be saved from the wrath of God through Him. For if while we were enemies we were reconciled to God through the death of His Son, much more, having been reconciled, we shall be saved by His life. And not only this, but we also celebrate in God through our Lord Jesus Christ, through whom we have now received the reconciliation.

Romans 10:8–9
But what does it say? "The word is near you, in your mouth and in your heart"—that is, the word of faith which we are preaching, that if you confess with your mouth Jesus as Lord,

The Helmet of Salvation

and believe in your heart that God raised Him from the dead, you will be saved.

Romans 8:13
For "Everyone who calls on the name of the Lord will be saved."

John 3:16–17
For God so loved the world, that He gave His only Son, so that everyone who believes in Him will not perish, but have eternal life. 17 For God did not send the Son into the world to judge the world, but so that the world might be saved through Him.

The laws of God are an extension of His charcter and nature and are designed for our benefit. Sin (Hebrew *ḥata'*—an archery term meaning to "miss the mark," fall short of the target) violates those laws. Sin is so antithetical to the order of heaven, that the justice of God requires a death penalty.

However, in God the Father's mercy and lovingkindness, He provided a substitute for us by taking on human flesh and paying the penalty for sin in our place. We need a Savior to be saved; or to put it another way, we need a "MESSiah" to clean up our mess!

How is salvation received?

Acts 2:38
Peter said to them, "Repent, and each of you be baptized in the name of Jesus Christ for the forgiveness of your sins; and you will receive the gift of the Holy Spirit.

Ephesians 2:8-9
For by grace you have been saved through faith; and that not of yourselves, it is the gift of God; not as a result of works, so that no one may boast.

Romans 10:8–10
But what does it say? "The word is near you, in your mouth and in your heart"—that is, the word of faith which we are

preaching, that if you confess with your mouth Jesus as Lord, and believe in your heart that God raised Him from the dead, you will be saved; for with the heart a person believes, resulting in righteousness, and with the mouth he confesses, resulting in salvation.

Salvation cannot be earned. It is a gift from God, not something we obtain through doing enough of the right actions, thereby obligating God to give it to us. Repentance is essential for salvation. What does it mean to repent? The Hebrew word we translate as "repentance" in English is *teshuva* (pronounced teh-SHOO-vuh). Teshuva is much more than simply a feeling of regret or guilt. The word comes from the verb meaning "to return."

When many people hear the word "repentance," they interpret it as meaning feeling sorry or feeling badly about something they've done. In that way, repentance becomes more of a feeling and less of an action. The problem with this misunderstanding is that one begins to feel tormented by regret that never seems to end.

Biblically, repentance has a wholly different focus. It's a decision rather than a state of mind. It's making a decision to change direction. You were headed the wrong way, and now you will turn back to God.

> Teshuva is returning to what is right and pure. It is returning to innocence. Aside from showing regret and remorse, it is returning to the original plan of God. To live with Him, consult with Him, fellowship with Him, and obey Him.
>
> So, essentially, to repent means to recognize our own wrongdoing and – humbly denying oneself – to turn around and face the One we have wronged. It is regretting our sin and showing remorse, yes. And it is also committing to a new path. Because this return path of correction and truth leads to true freedom. "to return."
>
> ...The process of repentance only makes sense if there

is a place we can return to. And that was made possible thanks to Jesus, our Messiah. He opened the doors for us to return to the Father. So, if teshuva means 'returning', then instead of dreading it, it can become the most beautiful experience for every believer.[3]

Joel 2:12
"Even now," declares the LORD, "return to me with all your heart …"

Repentance means despising our sins, turning away from them, asking God's forgiveness, and putting our trust in Jesus and His sacrifice on the cross. Then, we become obedient to God's laws—His *mitzvot*, commandments—in response. Our works or good deeds do not earn our salvation in any way. God, in His mercy, chose to pay the penalty for our sins.

1 John 5:13
These things I have written to you who believe in the name of the Son of God, so that you may know that you have eternal life. The apostle John reassures us that we can know we have eternal life, to live forever in God's presence. This is having the assurance of salvation.

1 John 5:11–12
And the testimony is this, that God has given us eternal life, and this life is in His Son. He who has the Son has the life; he who does not have the Son of God does not have the life.

We are promised life if we have Jesus. Without Jesus, we do not have life. Eternal life is a gift from God, carefully wrapped in the righteousness of His Son. When we accept and receive Jesus the Messiah and His

---

3. Wieja, Estera. "What Did Jesus Mean by Repent? The Hebrew Meaning of Teshuva." FIRM Israel, January 18, 2023. https://firmisrael.org/learn/what-did-jesus-mean-by-repent-the-hebrew-meaning-of-teshuva/.

righteousness, we are receiving life. Turning away from Jesus is akin to turning our backs on heaven itself.

This unwavering faith is the reason why believers hold the certainty of going to heaven. If the path to heaven depended on our own efforts, it would forever be uncertain and unattainable. However, when heaven is bestowed as a free gift, our assurance is unwavering because God's promises are sure. Just as we have received the perfect goodness of Jesus and surrendered our failures and sins to Him, eternal life with God becomes ours.

Donned in the breastplate of Jesus' righteousness, we can have absolute confidence in our eternal destiny. With the helmet of the hope of salvation securely in place, we are ready to confront the storms of life.

Indeed, life is difficult and full of challenges. That's an expected reality for followers of a crucified King. We grapple with internal struggles and external trials, which is all the more reason to be clad in the protective armor. When we face trials wearing the armor of God, and the forces of darkness have done their worst, when the theater of war is over, we will stand resolutely, buoyed by hope and empowered by the Holy Spirit.

Above all, safeguarding our minds, as symbolized by the helmet of salvation, is paramount. But why does it seem as if Paul advises us to put it on repeatedly? Do we remove our salvation before bedtime? No, because salvation (or justification) is a one-time event; we need not recite the sinner's prayer repeatedly until it sticks.

Remember, 1 Thessalonians 5:8 describes this armor piece as the "helmet of the *hope* of salvation." Salvation is something the Lord bestows upon us. It isn't something we can put on; the Lord Himself puts it on us. However, *hope* is a daily choice *we* make.

The devil often sows doubts about our salvation, introduces worldly distractions, and redirects our focus from eternity to current circumstances. The helmet of salvation acts as our protective gear, especially in the battlefield of the mind where Satan can deliver crushing blows. If we are plagued by doubts about our eternal standing, our vulnerability increases on the battlefield, leaving us incapable of spreading the gospel with the sword of the Spirit as we tend to our head injuries.

The Helmet of Salvation

The assurance of salvation forms our impenetrable defense against whatever the enemy hurls at us. As Jesus stated, *"Do not fear those who kill the body but are unable to kill the soul; but rather fear Him who is able to destroy both soul and body in hell"* (Matthew 10:28).

This verse underscores the importance of strapping on that helmet tightly as we prepare for Satan's attacks. It signifies that we should not fear physical harm, for this mortal body is temporary. Instead, our concern should be to please and honor God, the One who holds the keys to eternal life and death.

Salvation extends beyond a past event or a future hope; it's an ongoing, eternal state enjoyed by God's children in the present. It serves as our daily protection and deliverance from our sinful nature and the schemes of Satan.

Before entering any battlefield (realizing that every day *is* a spiritual battlefield) we must ensure we put on this helmet. How do we do that? By refreshing our minds daily through Scripture, with prayer in all circumstances, and remembering that the ultimate victory belongs to the Lord.

Satan's desire is to keep us ensnared in the present, where we witness tragic events on the news, grapple with doubts, and fear that we've lost our salvation. In such times, we must renew our trust in the Lord, confident that He will never forsake us.

Does salvation have to be continually maintained or is it an irrevocable gift?

Scripture informs us of three aspects of salvation: that we *"have* been saved" (Ephesians 2:5), that we *"are* being saved" (1 Corinthians 1:18) and that we *"will be* saved" (Matthew 10:22). What meaning does that have for us?

> **Ephesians 2:4-8**
> *But God, being rich in mercy, because of His great love with which He loved us, even when we were dead in our transgressions, made us alive together with Christ (by grace you have been saved), and raised us up with Him, and seated us*

> *with Him in the heavenly places in Christ Jesus, so that in the ages to come He might show the surpassing riches of His grace in kindness toward us in Christ Jesus. For by grace you have been saved through faith; and that not of yourselves, it is the gift of God...*

Paul explains that "have been saved" is equal to having our sins forgiven and coming under God's grace. The death penalty has been removed from us.

> **1 Corinthians 1:18 (KJV)**
> *For the preaching of the cross is to them that perish foolishness; but unto us which are saved it is the power of God.*

Salvation is also described as the ongoing process of sanctification. This is being "transformed by the renewing of your mind," as Paul writes in Romans 12:2. Sanctification encompasses having God's laws put in our hearts and written on our minds (Hebrews 10:16) and meditating on them as we go about our day. Doing so enables us to follow God's ways.

> **Psalm 119:97-99**
> *How I love Your Law!*
> *It is my meditation all the day.*
> *Your commandments make me wiser than my enemies,*
> *For they are ever mine.*
> *I have more insight than all my teachers,*
> *For Your testimonies are my meditation.*

As discussed in the chapter on the breastplate of righteousness, it's clear that God expects obedience to His commandments as a fruit of our salvation, and ultimately our salvation depends—not upon our works—but on our enduring to the end.

> **Matthew 10:22**
> *And you will be hated by all because of My name, but it is the one who has endured to the end who will be saved.*

The Helmet of Salvation

Thanks to the transformative power of the cross, Satan's grip on us has been broken. He is aware of this, but many of God's children may not fully grasp this truth or live accordingly. Therefore, we must learn to keep our salvation helmet firmly fastened, preventing the enemy's fiery darts from infiltrating our thoughts and igniting doubt.

With the helmet of salvation, *"We are destroying arguments and all arrogance raised against the knowledge of God, and we are taking every thought captive to the obedience of Christ"* (2 Corinthians 10:5).

Several essential actions can be taken by believers to ensure the helmet remains secure and functional. GotQuestions.org lists five keys:

1. Renew our minds.
2. Reject doubts that arise from circumstances.
3. Keep an eternal perspective.
4. Remember that victory is already accomplished.
5. Find all our hope in Him.

Adapted from the article:

> **Renew our minds:** Our minds serve as battlegrounds where the outcomes of these mental conflicts shape our lives. We are advised in Romans 12:1–2 not to conform to the world but to be transformed by renewing our minds. This involves replacing old, worldly perspectives with God's truth, cleansing our minds of impurities, lies, and confusion.
>
> **Reject doubts stemming from circumstances:** Human nature often relies on the senses, which may lead to doubts when faced with the intangible. The helmet of salvation empowers us to choose faith over doubt and reminds us of the joy that faith brings:
>
> > **Hebrews 11:6**
> > *And without faith it is impossible to please Him, for the one who comes to God must believe that He exists, and that He*

proves to be One who rewards those who seek Him.

1 Peter 1:8–9
And though you have not seen Him, you love Him, and though you do not see Him now, but believe in Him, you greatly rejoice with joy inexpressible and full of glory, obtaining as the outcome of your faith, the salvation of your souls.

Faith and doubt cannot coexist. James warns against being double-minded (James 1:8, 4:8). We can choose to have faith even in dire circumstances when we have the helmet of salvation securely buckled on.

Maintain an eternal perspective: When life's storms rage, it's crucial to lift our gaze upward. Our salvation is an invaluable gift, and keeping it in focus helps us weather life's trials. The motto "If it doesn't have eternal significance, it's not important" can guide our lives.

Recognize the victory already won: When we see ourselves as "dead to sin but alive to God" (Romans 6:11), we remove many of the avenues Satan exploits. Understanding our identity as "new creatures" eliminates sinful choices and blocks many roads to failure.

Place all hope in Him: Psalm 73:25 underscores the importance of treasuring God above all else. When we prioritize pleasing the Lord, Satan's temptations lose their power. When we cherish what the helmet of the hope of salvation symbolizes, it effectively guards our minds (GotQuestions, 2014).[4]

By wearing the helmet of salvation daily, our minds become

---

4. "What Is the Helmet of Salvation." GotQuestions.org, September 4, 2014. https://www.gotquestions.org/helmet-of-salvation.html.

The Helmet of Salvation

increasingly shielded against the enemy's schemes. We must deliberately guard our minds from excessive worldly influences and focus on thoughts that align with what is honorable, right, pure, lovely, commendable, and praiseworthy, as instructed in Philippians 4:8. In doing so, we experience the peace of God, guarding our hearts and minds in Christ Jesus.

8

The Shield of Faith

In addition to all, taking up the shield of faith with which you will be able to extinguish all the flaming arrows of the evil one.
Ephesians 6:16

In the shadow of imminent death, the trio of young men faced the searing reality of disobedience to the king's decree. A colossal furnace, heated sevenfold, awaited them—a brutal consequence for defying the monarch's command to worship a towering golden statue.

Moments earlier, the opportunity to evade this fate had presented itself, a mere surrender to save their lives. Yet, Shadrach, Meshach, and Abednego stood resolute, challenging the king's demand. The audacity lay not only in their defiance, but in their unwavering commitment to the God of Abraham, Isaac, and Jacob.

King Nebuchadnezzar's golden idol loomed over the nation, a symbol of his power and his subjects' submission. Yet, these three men, named for their courage, chose the path less traveled. Confronted by the king, they declared their unyielding faith: "Our God whom we serve is able to deliver us… but if not, we do not serve your gods." (Daniel 3:13–16).

Their journey from fierce loyalty to God into the fiery furnace became a testament to unshakeable faith, a faith that defied even the world's most powerful ruler. The miraculous intervention of God spared them from harm, but it was their unflinching dedication in the face of the unknown that defined their extraordinary story.

Transitioning to the metaphorical battlefield, the narrative shifts to the shield—the protective gear in the arsenal of God. Unlike the armor worn, the shield demands action; it is not a passive defense. The belt, breastplate, and shoes are items worn on the body; however, the shield is something that needs to be taken up. Just securing it to one's arm does no good; it must be held up and moved to be effective.

The Roman *scutum* was a massive rectangular shield about three-and-a-half feet tall and almost three feet wide. It was curved slightly and had a large metal knob in the center, called a "boss." Its curvature offered substantial protection and the ability to deflect blows without overwhelming the bearer. Furthermore, the boss could be used offensively to thrust an opponent backward.

Yet, as protective as the shield was, it was of considerable weight and too large for soldiers on horseback. Mounted warriors wielded the Parma—a smaller, rounded shield designed for agility and adaptability. Crafted from either iron, wood, or leather, the Parma was up to 36-inches in size.

The soldier's arsenal included a variety of shields for different uses. Similarly, the shield of faith must be applied with wisdom, tailored to the nuances of life's varied circumstances.

Defining faith through a biblical lens, Hebrews 11:1 designates faith as the tangible substance of hope and the solid evidence of the unseen. Faith, far from a mystical abstraction, is portrayed as the irrefutable truth, grounded in reality. Romans 8:24-25 further illustrates faith as the force that propels us forward, eagerly awaiting the unseen with perseverance and expectation.

Hebrews 11:1 (KJV)
Now faith is the substance of things hoped for, the evidence of things not seen.

The Shield of Faith

Romans 8:24-25
For in hope we have been saved, but hope that is seen is not hope; for who hopes for what he already sees? But if we hope for what we do not see, through perseverance we wait eagerly for it.

We operate on a daily basis with faith; it's just a matter of recognizing it. The word faith is often interchangeable with the words "trust" and "confidence." We get up in the morning and trust—or have faith—that the chair we sit down on at the breakfast table is going to hold us up. We have faith that our car will start so we can get to work. This is the kind of faith that is so natural we don't give it a second thought. So, faith is not just some mystical, foggy belief that something is real.

The important thing to remember here is that faith is only as good and trustworthy as the object in which it is placed. For a period of time in my life, I placed my faith in Mormonism and its founder Joseph Smith, Jr.. I trusted and believed it was true. In reality, what I had was wishful thinking, because I didn't test the object of my belief. Upon close examination, the whole concept and structure of Mormonism crumbled.

Bible teacher Chuck Missler wrote:

> Faith should be a response to proven truth. Any faith which is not based upon reason supported by irrefutable evidence is the utmost folly. Gullibility is no help to true faith but is actually its enemy. Skepticism is, in fact, essential as the first step toward true faith, so long as it doesn't harden into pride or become a cloak for prejudice. No thinking person can embrace just "any god" as the Creator of the universe; the same Creator who has a purpose in our existence and who holds us accountable:

> **Hebrews 11:6** *But without faith it is impossible to please Him: for he that cometh to God must believe that He is, and that He is a rewarder of them that diligently seek Him.*

No one can have faith in God—that is, absolute and total trust in Him—without knowing Him. Thus, the path to growing your faith is simply to learn more of Him.

How does one do that? First, by discovering the majesty and integrity of His Word, giving it its proper priority in your life. Second, by maintaining a continuing dialog with Him in your life (Missler, 1996).[1]

It's imperative that we understand and know what are we are placing our faith in. Faith requires a large dose of trust. As with anything of importance, examining the evidence is a must. In terms of our belief and reliance on God of the Bible, we can see from Scripture that God is faithful and unchangeable, and that we can trust Him to fulfill all His promises to us.

Have you ever heard the expression "good faith?" It means honesty, fairness, and lawfulness of purpose: absence of any intent to defraud, act maliciously, or take unfair advantage; for instance, to bargain in good faith. Here is the legal definition:

> The meaning of good faith, though always based on honesty, may vary depending on the specific context in which it is used. A person is said to buy in good faith when he or she holds an honest belief in his or her right or title to the property and has no knowledge or reason to know of any defect in the title (Merriam-Webster, n.d.).[2]

We come to God in good faith that if we accept His terms of repentance and confession, He will justify us through the blood of Jesus Christ. Let's look at **Romans 10:8–9**:

> *[8]But what does it say? "The word is near you, in your mouth and in your heart"—that is, the word of faith which*

---

1. Missler, Chuck. "The Shield of Faith: The Armor of God." Koinonia House. December 1, 1996. https://www.khouse.org/articles/1996/268/.
2. "Good Faith - Findlaw Dictionary of Legal Terms." FindLaw Legal Dictionary. Accessed February 25, 2024. https://dictionary.findlaw.com/definition/good-faith.html.

*we are preaching, ⁹that **if you confess** with your mouth Jesus as Lord, and believe in your heart that God raised Him from the dead, **you will be saved*** [emphasis mine].

The same verses from the Complete Jewish Bible:

*⁸What, then, does it say? 'The word is near you in your mouth and in your heart.' that is, the word about trust which we proclaim, namely, ⁹that **if you acknowledge** publicly with your mouth that Yeshua is Lord and trust in your heart that God raised him from the dead, **you will be delivered*** [emphasis mine].

We see those same interchangeable words: *faith* and *trust*. Where verse 8 says, *"What, then, does it say? 'The word is near you in your mouth and in your heart,'"* it's referring to **Deuteronomy 30:11-14**:

*For this commandment which I am commanding you today is not too difficult for you, nor is it far away. It is not in heaven, that you could say, 'Who will go up to heaven for us and get it for us, and proclaim it to us, so that we may follow it?' Nor is it beyond the sea, that you could say, 'Who will cross the sea for us and get it for us and proclaim it to us, so that we may follow it?' On the contrary, the word is very near you, **in your mouth and in your heart**, that you may follow it* [emphasis mine].

In other words, God doesn't require us to build a tower to heaven to reach Him, or to seek out some guru across the ocean to find someone to teach us truth. We have His word right here with us, written in Scripture and written on our hearts.

Ephesians 2:8
For by grace you have been saved through faith, and that not of yourselves; it is the gift of God.

1 Corinthians 12:7–9
But to each one is given the manifestation of the Spirit for the common good. For to one is given the word of wisdom through the Spirit, and to another the word of knowledge according to the same Spirit; to another faith by the same Spirit, and to another gifts of healing by the one Spirit…

Faith is both a gift and an act of our will. We make a free-will choice to place our trust in Jesus and His blood shed on the cross. Faith is not an ooey-gooey feeling; it's putting trust into action, putting our money where our mouth is, in a manner of speaking.

We give everything we have to Jesus, and He gives more than that back to us. Would you trade all your earthly possessions for a billion dollars? It's like God says, "I'll give you a billion dollars for that hundred dollar bill." And you're like, "What hundred dollar bill?" And He reaches into His pocket and says, "This hundred dollar bill," as He puts it into your hand. God asks for our faith, and then He gives us the faith we need as a gift!

The association of a shield with faith is profound and multifaceted. Just as a physical shield provides protection, faith serves as a spiritual safeguard amid physical trials. Shadrach, Meshach, and Abednego exemplify this, standing unwavering against Satan's assault through Nebuchadnezzar on their values; their faith a resolute defense.

In their response to the king's threat, they declared in essence, "God is capable of delivering us… but that doesn't matter. He gave us His commands, and we will keep them regardless of the outcome. We know He can raise us from the dead if He chooses."

Ephesians 6:16 emphasizes the shield of faith, a crucial defense against Satan's fiery darts—fear, doubt, and worry. When our shield of faith remains raised, these assaults are deflected, preserving our confidence in God's control and the ultimate good He has for us, good that He brings out of even the most awful of circumstances.

That's a hard concept. But we have to realize that there are many moving parts. God loves each of us intensely, personally. And He cares deeply about each and every one of us. However, not everything is all about us individually. God is the only one who sees the whole picture and every moving part of it.

He sees all the tomorrows and how every event, every choice, every action not only impacts the present, but how it will impact the future. He sees what we do not. He sees what the ripples in the pond lead to. The things we see as hardships or tragedy, we can trust that He will bring good out of it somehow, in some way, at some point to rescue as many souls as possible, bringing redemption to the penitent and to bring justice and righteous judgment to the wicked. It's imperative that we have confidence in our Lord and Savior:

> **Matthew 14:28-31**
> *And Peter answered Him and said, "Lord, if it is You, command me to come to You on the water." So He said, "Come." And when Peter had come down out of the boat, he walked on the water to go to Jesus. But when he saw that the wind was boisterous, he was afraid; and beginning to sink he cried out, saying, "Lord, save me!" And immediately Jesus stretched out His hand and caught him, and said to him, "O you of little faith, why did you doubt?"*

A shield is the initial line of defense—and faith, when strong, prevents Satan from breaking through. Doubt, as seen with Peter on the waves, leads to spiritual fatigue, battering both the believer and their armor. An actively raised shield of faith prevents this weariness.

Jesus, with unwavering purpose, repelled Satan, emphasizing the power of faith in God's Word and commands:

> **Matthew 4:10-11 (CJB)**
> *Away with you, Satan!" Yeshua told him, "For the Tanakh says, 'Worship Adonai your God, and serve only him.'"*
> *Then the Adversary let him alone, and angels came and took care of him.*

> **Luke 4:13**
> *When the Adversary had ended all his testings, he let him alone until an opportune time.*

Yeshua's testing in the wilderness was not the only time He encountered Satan, for **Hebrews 4:15** tells us;

> *For we do not have a high priest who cannot sympathize with our weaknesses, but* ***One who has been tempted in all things just as we are****, yet without sin* (Emphasis mine).

The shield repels attacks. It incapacitates, giving believers a chance to fight back against the darkness by doing God's will and work. James 2:20 highlights that faith must produce actions. Christ's faith (His complete trust in the Father), as demonstrated in resisting temptation, parallels the Roman shield's boss, allowing for a counterattack that pushes back against spiritual adversaries.

Beyond individual faith, the shields of many find strength in unity. Combining faith with others fortifies the entire body of Christ. Like the Roman *testudo*—or tortoise—formation, where soldiers interlock their shields for impregnable defense, united faith strengthens believers collectively. When we combine our faith with the faith of others, we strengthen and bless the whole body of Christ.

Ephesians 4:11-16
And He gave some as apostles, some as prophets, some as evangelists, some as pastors and teachers, for the equipping of the saints for the work of ministry, for the building up of the body of Christ; until we all attain to the unity of the faith, and of the knowledge of the Son of God, to a mature man, to the measure of the stature which belongs to the fullness of Christ.

As a result, we are no longer to be children, tossed here and there by waves and carried about by every wind of doctrine, by the trickery of people, by craftiness in deceitful scheming; but speaking the truth in love, we are to grow up in all aspects into Him who is the head, that is, Christ, from whom the whole body, being fitted and held together by what every joint supplies, according to the proper working of each individual part, causes the growth of the body for the building up of itself in love.

Just as the Roman infantry adapted tactics and formations for battle, believers must apply faith strategically. Consideration of circumstances, opponents, and terrain, akin to the Romans' strategic approach, ensures a resilient defense against spiritual adversaries.

In uniting faith and utilizing strategic spiritual formations, believers become a formidable force—akin to a walking tank, impervious to the assaults of doubt and our spiritual foes. The battle is not ours alone as individuals, but we fight against the powers of darkness for all our brothers and sisters in the faith around the world in preparation for the return of Yeshua Hamashiach—Jesus our King!

9

The Sword of the Spirit

For the word of God is living and active, and sharper than any two-edged sword, even penetrating as far as the division of soul and spirit, of both joints and marrow, and able to judge the thoughts and intentions of the heart.
Hebrews 4:12

Judges 7 records the remarkable story of Gideon and his battle against Israel's enemy. Gideon and his military contingent of 32,000 Israelite troops gathered near the Midianite encampment, facing daunting odds against their 135,000 oppressors. Gideon's resolve to engage in battle was unwavering, but divine intervention was in the making. God had a remarkable demonstration of His power in store for His people.

In a surprising twist, God instructed Gideon to allow anyone afraid to face the impending battle to return home. A staggering 22,000 men chose to depart, leaving a mere 10,000 standing. But God sought an even smaller, more select group.

God then directed Gideon to have the remaining men drink from a spring, and those who lapped the water like dogs were chosen to stay, while the others were sent home. With a minuscule force of only 300 men, Gideon and his modest army encircled the Midianites. At a predetermined signal, they sounded their trumpets, shattered the pitchers covering their torches, and proclaimed, "The sword of the Lord and of Gideon!" (Judges 7:20).

What transpired next was beyond imagination. These 300 men, armed not with swords but with torches and trumpets, routed the entire Midianite camp. Scripture recounts that God "set every man's sword against his companion throughout the whole camp" (Judges 7:22). Even before the Israelites could draw their swords, God cast the enemy camp into turmoil and utter defeat. Through a miraculous intervention, the Israelites were delivered from their adversaries. This iconic tale serves as a profound lesson: Victory is granted by God, and it is His divine sword that ensures our deliverance.

Around the world, both real and fictional figures exist whose identity is nearly inseparable from their chosen weapon. Charlemagne, king of the Franks, was said to have won against the Saracens at the battle of Roncevaux with his double-edged sword, Joyeuse. In Spain, there's El Cid, whose trusty long sword was known as Tizona. Live theater, movies and literature are replete with stories of King Arthur and his legendary sword, Excalibur.

Interestingly, when considering the elements of armor mentioned by Paul, it's the sword that stands out as the sole offensive tool. All others parts of the armor are for defensive purposes. The belt, helmet, breastplate, shoes and greaves, and shield are invaluable to us in providing for our defense; however, the absence of the sword makes us vulnerable to injury, for not only is a sword a tool to disarm an opponent, but it also works as a secondary shield with which to ward off blows.

Paul lists "the sword of the Spirit, which is the word of God" as the sixth piece of armor. The imagery of a soldier's sword helps us understand that God's word is active and powerful, and is of great use in becoming victorious when engaged in our spiritual battle against the forces of evil.

History records there were five different types of swords that were used by Roman soldiers, the most notable of which was the *gladius*, a long-bladed sword, that although beautifully crafted, was so heavy and cumbersome that a soldier of neccessity used two hands to wield it. However, it was the later-developed *machaira* that was the deadliest of all the swords available to the infantrymen.

The Sword of the Spirit

According to Rick Renner in his book, *Dressed to Kill: A Biblical Approach to Spiritual Warfare and Armor*:

> This brutal weapon of murder was approximately 19-inches long. Both sides of its blade were razor sharp, making this sword much more dangerous than the other four. In addition, the tip of the sword turned upward, causing the point of the blade to be extremely sharp and deadly.
>
> This two edged blade inflicted a wound far worse than the other swords. Before a Roman soldier withdrew this particular sword from the gut of his enemy, he would hold his sword very tightly with both hands and give it a wrenching twist inside his enemy's stomach. This would cause the opponents entrails to spill out as the soldier pulled the sword from his enemy's body.
>
> Of all the swords available, this machaira sword was the most dangerous of all. Although the other swords were deadly, this one was a terror to the imagination! This sword was not only intended to kill, but to completely rip an enemy's insides to shreds. It was a weapon of murder! Because Paul uses the word *machaira* in Ephesians 6:17 to describe our "sword of the Spirit," he declares that God has given the Church a weapon that is just as brutal against our enemy! This weapon, called "sword of the Spirit," has the potential to rip our foe to shreds! (Renner, 2013).[1]

Renner goes on to say that believers don't need to commit entire Bible passages or a good portion of verses to memory in order to be used by God or for Him to speak to them. While it's a good practice

---

[1]. Renner, Rick. Dressed to Kill. Destiny Image Publishers, 2013.

to memorize Scripture, it's the sword of the Spirit that we have at our disposal. In other words, the Holy Spirit will speak *to* us and *through* us, bringing to mind the word of God in those critical moments of need because of the living and active nature of His Word:

> **Hebrews 4:12**
> *For the word of God is living and active, sharper than any two-edged sword, piercing to the division of soul and of spirit, of joints and of marrow, and discerning the thoughts and intentions of the heart.*

Jesus prayed to the Father, "Sanctify them by Your truth. Your word is truth" (John 17:17). This assures us that the written and Incarnate Word of God is synonymous with truth. Hearing and obeying the Word of God brings blessings, as stated in **Luke 11:28**:

> *But He said, "On the contrary, blessed are those who hear the word of God and observe it."*

Isaiah 55:10-11 declares that God's Word accomplishes its purpose without fail, just as the rain and snow nurture the earth and yield a harvest:

> *For as the rain and the snow come down from heaven,*
> *And do not return there without watering the earth*
> *And making it produce and sprout,*
> *And providing seed to the sower and bread to the eater;*
> *So will My word be which goes out of My mouth;*
> *It will not return to Me empty,*
> *Without accomplishing what I desire,*
> *And without succeeding in the purpose for which I sent it.*

The word of God gives us light. The word of God, whether in written or spoken form, offers illumination and guidance, revealing both the wise and the unwise paths to life. It empowers individuals to navigate life without stumbling in the darkness:

Psalm 119:105
Your word is a lamp to my feet and a light to my path.

At its core, the Word of God is truth and possesses profound power, both in spiritual warfare and in lighting the path to a purposeful life.

The Imagery of the Sword in Scripture.

The formidable sword of the Almighty, wielded by servants of God, possesses the unmatched ability to cut through every defense the enemy erects, reaching deep into the very essence of the matter to reveal the truth. As soldiers in God's army, we bear the sacred duty of employing His Word to discern truth and, when necessary, to skillfully excise errors of doctrine and practice.

The weapons of spiritual warfare are powerful because they are divine. Paul delineates the divine potency of this spiritual weaponry:

2 Corinthians 10:4-5
For the weapons of our warfare are not of the flesh, but divinely powerful for the destruction of fortresses. We are destroying arguments and all arrogance raised against the knowledge of God, and we are taking every thought captive to the obedience of Christ.

In contrast to the defensive nature of the other elements of God's armor, the sword stands alone as an instrument for both defense and offense. While a solid defense is invaluable, the sword is our means to fulfill the work the Lord entrusted to us.

This weapon also serves as our vanguard against the lies of the Adversary. Picture two opponent warriors in combat, swords clanging as they meet blade to blade. Satan knows Scripture, perhaps better than we do; however, he twists it to try to gain advantage. It's written that Satan is the "father of lies." Speaking of Satan, Jesus said:

John 8:44
He was a murderer from the beginning, and does not stand in

the truth because there is no truth in him. Whenever he tells a lie, he speaks from his own nature, because he is a liar and the father of lies.

In countering Satan's attacks, Jesus employed the truth of Scripture. When tempted by Satan, He responded with the Word of God:

Matthew 4:1–11 (NLT)
Then Jesus was led by the Spirit into the wilderness to be tempted there by the devil. For forty days and forty nights he fasted and became very hungry.

During that time the devil came and said to him, "If you are the Son of God, tell these stones to become loaves of bread."

But Jesus told him, "No! The Scriptures say,

> *'People do not live by bread alone, but by every word that comes from the mouth of God.'"*

Then the devil took him to the holy city, Jerusalem, to the highest point of the Temple, and said, "If you are the Son of God, jump off! For the Scriptures say,

> *'He will order his angels to protect you.*
> *And they will hold you up with their hands so you won't even hurt your foot on a stone.'"*

Jesus responded, "The Scriptures also say, 'You must not test the Lord your God.'"

Next the devil took him to the peak of a very high mountain and showed him all the kingdoms of the world and their glory.
"I will give it all to you," he said, "if you will kneel down and worship me."

The Shield of Faith

"Get out of here, Satan," Jesus told him. "For the Scriptures say, 'You must worship the Lord your God and serve only him.'"

Then the devil went away, and angels came and took care of Jesus.

We, too, must learn to live "by every word that proceeds from the mouth of God."

As followers of Jesus, the battle we face is typically "up close and personal." Assaults to our faith come in various forms and hit the most vulnerable parts of our lives: relationships, health, finances, and self-worth and confidence. We suffer from loss, doubts, stress, rejection, and persecution among other issues that are part and parcel of living in a broken world.

The choice of a sword, typically used in close combat, implies the nature of the battle we face. Scripture indicates the trials and tribulations inherent in the path of entering the kingdom of God:

> **Acts 14:21–22**
> *And after they had preached the gospel to that city and had made a good number of disciples, they returned to Lystra, to Iconium, and to Antioch, strengthening the souls of the disciples, encouraging them to continue in the faith, and saying, **"It is through many tribulations that we must enter the kingdom of God."** [Emphasis mine]*

The Tree of Life version translates it as this:

> *"It is through many **persecutions** that we must enter the kingdom of God."*

No one likes going through rough times or painful experiences, yet, the value of trials is that—if endured well—they shape our faith and character:

James 1:2–4
My brethren, count it all joy when you fall into various trials, knowing that the testing of your faith produces patience. But let patience have its perfect work, that you may be perfect and complete, lacking nothing.

To maximize the effectiveness of a sword, a soldier must be trained in its use. Similarly, we must be trained in the Word of God. This involves committing Scripture to memory, prayer, and cultivating sensitivity to the Holy Spirit. A solid understanding of our spiritual weapon equips us for battle. Bible expositor Matthew Henry explained in his commentary:

> To the Christian armed for defense in battle, the apostle recommends only one weapon of attack; but it is enough, the sword of the Spirit, which is the word of God. It subdues and mortifies evil desires and blasphemous thoughts as they rise within; and answers unbelief and error as they assault from without. A single text, well understood, and rightly applied, at once destroys a temptation or an objection, and subdues the most formidable adversary.[2]

As *Matthew Henry's Concise Commentary* emphasizes, the sword of the Spirit, which is the word of God, subdues evil desires, blasphemous thoughts, unbelief, and error. It stands as a formidable tool to address temptations and objections.

However, we must exercise caution in wielding the sword of the Spirit, for misuse can place us in spiritual peril on the battlefield. Whether used for offensive evangelism or defensive apologetics, comprehensive understanding of God's Word is vital.

Pastor and teacher Jamie Walden noted that a policeman without his car and gun is nothing. Neither is a fire fighter without his gear, or paramedic without his kit. A soldier without weapons or artillery

---

2. Matthew Henry's Concise Commentary, retrieved from https://biblehub.com/commentaries/ephesians/6-11.htm

is a sitting duck. These professionals must be properly equipped to be effective in performing their duties.

Likewise, a soldier in God's Kingdom who isn't equipped with the sword of the Spirit will not survive the days ahead—and I'm not just referring to physical survival—I'm talking primarily about spiritual survival. If we don't know God intimately and aren't confident in our identity in Christ, we're at great risk of falling away from the faith. A government can disarm its citizens, but it cannot spiritually disarm a remnant warrior in full "supernatural" kit, unless the Christian lays down the sword and takes off his armor.

How do we use the Bible properly to *a)* spread the Gospel and *b)* be prepared for any questions or doubts that may arise regarding Scripture? How are we to properly utilize Scripture to spread the gospel message and to be ready to answer questions that may arise concerning the veracity of the Bible?

1. Read the Word in its Context.

When wielding the Sword, it's essential to avoid any misinterpretation by considering the original context. We must avoid the error of reading into the text our own cultural bias. Take Philippians 4:13, for example, "I can do all things through Christ who strengthens me."

This verse doesn't mean you can go "faster than a speeding bullet and leap tall buildings in a single bound," or get that exciting job promotion because Jesus is giving you the might to do so. Rather than misusing it for personal pursuits, understanding the context is vital.

Paul, who suffered in prison with an unknown weakness he called a "thorn in the flesh," explained:

> **Philippians 4:11b–13**
> *For I have learned to be content in whatever circumstances I am. I know how to get along with little, and I also know how to live in prosperity; in any and every circumstance I have learned the secret of being filled and going hungry, both of having abundance and suffering need. I can do all things through Him who strengthens me.*

He is saying he can endure hardships through Messiah's strength. To use the Bible effectively, we must grasp the context of its passages.

2. Gaining Proficiency in Scripture.

To achieve proficiency, we need to immerse ourselves in God's Word on a regular basis. Reading the Bible, studying commentaries, and listening to solid Bible teachers provide a deeper understanding of Scripture. The apostle Peter instructs us:

1 Peter 3:15
[S]anctify Christ as Lord in your hearts, always being ready to make a defense to everyone who asks you to give an account for the hope that is in you, yet with gentleness and reverence.

It will be difficult to make a defense for our beliefs (known as apologetics) if we don't know our Bible, or at the very least, to have a basic understanding of what the gospel is and the many proofs for the Messiahship of Jesus. This is especially vital when answering questions or addressing challenges from individuals of different beliefs. By engaging with the written word daily, we can be prepared to spread the gospel and address inquiries effectively.

We see in Acts 8:26-40, an Ethiopian eunuch is reading from the scroll of the prophet Isaiah (Isaiah 53:7-8) and has trouble understanding it. Directed by an angel to meet the eunuch on the road descending from Jerusalem, Philip—a disciple of Jesus—runs alongside the chariot and is invited to sit with this court official. He's able to explain the passage from Isaiah, and the Ethiopian eunuch puts his trust in Jesus as the Messiah and is baptized in a nearby body of water. Wouldn't it be great to be so proficient in Scripture that we can explain it to those who have questions?

3. Asking God to Reveal Himself through His Word

God reveals Himself to us—His character, nature, and plan—in His word and through the Holy Spirit. By setting aside time each day to devote to prayer and His Word, we grow close to Him and develop a better understanding *of* and a greater trust *in* His purposes.

1 Corinthians 2:10-15
For to us God revealed them through the Spirit; for the Spirit searches all things, even the depths of God. For who among people knows the thoughts of a person except the spirit of the person that is in him? So also the thoughts of God no one knows, except the Spirit of God.

Now we have not received the spirit of the world, but the Spirit who is from God, so that we may know the things freely given to us by God. We also speak these things, not in words taught by human wisdom, but in those taught by the Spirit, combining spiritual thoughts with spiritual words.

But a natural person does not accept the things of the Spirit of God, for they are foolishness to him; and he cannot understand them, because they are spiritually discerned. But the one who is spiritual discerns all things, yet he himself is discerned by no one.

Jesus placed significant importance on God's Word. Our Messiah had high regard for the Hebrew Scriptures. He used Scripture to resist temptation and counter the devil's attacks. All His teachings sprang out of the Torah, and He made it clear that the writings of the prophets testified about Him:

John 5:39
You examine the Scriptures because you think that in them you have eternal life; and it is those very Scriptures that testify about Me.

John 17:17
Sanctify them in the truth; Your word is truth.

And the apostle Paul asserts that all Scripture serves a purpose:

2 Timothy 3:16
All Scripture is inspired by God and beneficial for teaching, for rebuke, for correction, for training in righteousness.

A sword is used as a symbol of divine punishment or correction in addition to embodying God's Word. At times, God wields His divine sword against those who defy His will, whether they be Israel's enemies or the wayward among His chosen people:

Psalm 7:12
If one does not repent, He will sharpen His sword; He has bent His bow and taken aim.

Psalm 78:62
He also turned His people over to the sword, And was filled with wrath at His inheritance.

As warriors and citizens of the Kingdom of Heaven, it's essential that we make it a priority to be familiar with His word and to seek to understand it. As **Hosea 4:6** warns;

My people are destroyed for lack of knowledge.
Because you have rejected knowledge,
I also will reject you from being My priest.
Since you have forgotten the law of your God,
I also will forget your children.

The Word of God possesses the power to pierce even the most obstinate hearts, bringing about life transformation. The Word of God is life—revealing God's truth and offering the gift of salvation through Jesus. The sword of the Spirit equips us to stand firm against the relentless attacks of our adversary, Satan. It empowers the Holy Spirit to rescue souls and fortify them as valiant soldiers in the battle against the corruption and evil that pervades our world. It also safeguards us and keeps our feet on His sure path:

Psalm 119:11
I have treasured Your word in my heart, So that I may not sin against You.

Promises are reserved for those who conquer, not for those who remain stagnant or abandon the fight. There is no personal and spiritual growth without trials, and as uncomfortable as they are to go through, they are essential for entering the kingdom of God.

Paul and Barnabas returned from a missionary journey, "strengthening the disciples, encouraging them to remain true to the faith, and **reminding them that it is through many hardships that we must enter the Kingdom of God**" (**Acts 14:22**). By persevering and enduring the hardships, we can anticipate the glorious rewards awaiting us.

Revelation 2:7, 11, 17, 26

V. 7 - *The one who has an ear, let him hear what the Spirit says to the churches. To the one who overcomes, I will grant to eat from the tree of life, which is in the Paradise of God.*

V. 11 - *The one who overcomes will not be hurt by the second death.*

V. 17 - *To the one who overcomes, I will give some of the hidden manna, and I will give him a white stone, and a new name written on the stone which no one knows except the one who receives it.*

V. 26 - *The one who overcomes, and the one who keeps My deeds until the end, I will give him authority over the nations;*

Revelation 3:5, 12, 21

V. 5 - *The one who overcomes will be clothed the same way, in white garments; and I will not erase his name from the book* *of life, and I will confess his name before My Father and before His angels.*

V. 12 - *The one who overcomes, I will make him a pillar in the temple of My God, and he will not go out from it anymore; and I will write on him the name of My God, and the name of the city of My God, the new Jerusalem, which comes down out of heaven from My God, and My new name.*

V. 21 - *The one who overcomes, I will grant to him to sit with Me on My throne, as I also overcame and sat with My Father on His throne. The one who has an ear, let him hear what the Spirit says to the churches.*

Matthew 24:13
But he who endures to the end shall be saved.

Among the pieces of the armor of God, Paul notes that only one weapon is necessary for offensive purposes. The Word of God, combined with the Holy Spirit, is all-encompassing and brings victory. Armed with this solitary offensive weapon, our sword, we confront our adversaries head-on.

The battle is real and ever-present, with the specter of sudden destruction looming on just about every front. In the midst of Babylon, we must heed the call to come out. Our future in God's Kingdom hinges on our commitment to this fight.

Though the journey may be arduous, we are to move forward with unwavering faith, for God's unshakable promises assure us of salvation. As **Isaiah 46:11** proclaims,

> *"Indeed I have spoken it; I will also bring it to pass. I have purposed it; I will also do it."*

So take up your sword. The battle is fierce, but victory is secured.

10

The Cloak of Zeal

He put on righteousness like a breastplate, And a helmet of salvation on His head; And He put on garments of vengeance for clothing And wrapped Himself with zeal as a cloak.
Isaiah 59:17

When I think of zeal, what comes to mind is Joshua and Caleb. Moses sent 12 men, one from each tribe of Israel, into the land of Canaan to spy out the area and find out a few things about it:

Numbers 13:17–20
When Moses sent them to spy out the land of Canaan, he said to them, "Go up there into the Negev; then go up into the hill country. See what the land is like, and whether the people who live in it are strong or weak, whether they are few or many. And how is the land in which they live, is it good or bad? And how are the cities in which they live, are the people in open camps or in fortifications? And how is the land, is it productive or unproductive? Are there trees in it or not? And show yourselves courageous and get some of the fruit of the land." Now the time was the season of the first ripe grapes.

The spies came back to Moses and the congregation of Israel after their 40-day reconnaissance mission. They had some exciting and alarming news:

Numbers 13:27–29
So they reported to him and said, "We came into the land where you sent us, and it certainly does flow with milk and honey, and this is its fruit. Nevertheless, the people who live in the land are strong, and the cities are fortified and very large. And indeed, we saw the descendants of Anak there! Amalek is living in the land of the Negev, the Hittites, the Jebusites, and the Amorites are living in the hill country, and the Canaanites are living by the sea and by the side of the Jordan."

This report was extremely disturbing to the Children of Israel because the Anakim were a fearsome race of giants—great, not only in terms of size, but in strength and military prowess. While we don't know exactly how large the Anakim or the Amorites were, they were large enough for the Israelites to seem like grasshoppers in size compared to them. No wonder the Israelites were scared witless! When they heard the report, a sound of dismay arose from the congregation.

Numbers 13:30–33
Then Caleb quieted the people before Moses and said, "We should by all means go up and take possession of it, for we will certainly prevail over it."

But the men who had gone up with him said, "We are not able to go up against the people, because they are too strong for us." So they brought a bad report of the land which they had spied out to the sons of Israel, saying, "The land through which we have gone to spy out is a land that devours its inhabitants; and all the people whom we saw in it are people of great stature. We also saw the Nephilim there (the sons of Anak are part of the Nephilim); and we were like grasshoppers in our own sight, and so we were in their sight."

The Cloak of Zeal

An uproar ensued among the people and they cried all night, lamenting that they had ever been led out of Egypt. They were clearly distraught and complained about their plight, speaking out against God, Moses, Aaron, and the two faithful spies.

> **Numbers 14:5–10**
> *Then Moses and Aaron fell on their faces in the presence of all the assembly of the congregation of the sons of Israel. And Joshua the son of Nun and Caleb the son of Jephunneh, of those who had spied out the land, tore their clothes; and they spoke to all the congregation of the sons of Israel, saying, "The land which we passed through to spy out is an exceedingly good land. If the Lord is pleased with us, then He will bring us into this land and give it to us—a land which flows with milk and honey. Only do not rebel against the Lord; and do not fear the people of the land, for they will be our prey. Their protection is gone from them, and the Lord is with us; do not fear them." But all the congregation said to stone them with stones.*

Even in the face of possibly being stoned to death by the angry mob, Caleb and Joshua remained resolute—zealous for carrying out the mission that God had prepared for His people. The 10 spies who brought a bad report and caused the people to grumble and disrespect the LORD died from a plague, and the Children of Israel were consigned to wander in the desert for 40 years until the older generations perished. Caleb and Joshua were rewarded for being zealous in trusting God and walking according to His will. These two faithful and trusting Israelites wore zeal as a cloak about them.

Although the apostle Paul did not include the cloak of zeal in his description of the armor of God, zeal is referenced in **Zechariah 8:2**:

> *Thus says the Lord of hosts: "I am zealous for Zion with great zeal; with great fervor I am zealous for her."*

The dictionary defines zeal it as:

Enthusiastic devotion to a cause, ideal, or goal.
Passionate ardor in the pursuit of anything; intense interest or endeavor; eagerness to accomplish or obtain some object.[1]

Examining its role in the Roman army, the cloak proves versatile—it provides warmth, repels rain with natural oils, and doubles as makeshift bedding during long marches. Deprived of their cloak, soldiers faced bitter cold, freezing rain, and uncomfortable nights, impacting their motivation and combat effectiveness.

Spiritually, zeal is similar to the soldier's cloak. It's the fervent passion driving individuals, their purpose, and what they live for as the remnant body of Christ. Without motivation and purpose, it's difficult for individuals to be effective in their life pursuits; how much more then for those professing belief in Yahweh? The cloak, mentioned in Isaiah, serves as a vital tool in the ongoing battle against Satan.

Isaiah 59:17
He put on righteousness like a breastplate, And a helmet of salvation on His head; And He put on garments of vengeance for clothing And wrapped Himself with zeal as a cloak.

The Creator Himself is zealous for His people and His ultimate plan for humanity. Zeal is the divine fuel that ignites the burning desire within remnant warriors to align their lives with God's will and purpose. It's the fervent passion that propels them forward, shaping their identity and motivating them to actively pursue the divine plan. In the grand tapestry of faith, zeal becomes the driving force, the unwavering commitment to live for something greater and to passionately fulfill God's purpose.

We see zeal demonstrated in Numbers 25. A plague had come upon Israel because many of them became involved in the worship of Ba'al. Ba'al worship involved sexual depravity, orgies, and the sacrifice of babies and young children. It was usually the first-born who was made

---

1. American Heritage® Dictionary of the English Language, Fifth Edition. S.v. "zeal." Retrieved January 20 2024 from https://www.thefreedictionary.com/zeal

to pass through the fire—in other words being burned alive.

> **Numbers 25:5-11**
> *So Moses said to the judges of Israel, "Every one of you kill his men who were joined to Baal of Peor."*
>
> *And indeed, one of the children of Israel came and presented to his brethren a Midianite woman in the sight of Moses and in the sight of all the congregation of the children of Israel, who were weeping at the door of the tabernacle of meeting.*
>
> *Now when Phinehas the son of Eleazar, the son of Aaron the priest, saw it, he rose from among the congregation and took a javelin in his hand; and he went after the man of Israel into the tent and thrust both of them through, the man of Israel, and the woman through her body.*
>
> *So the plague was stopped among the children of Israel. And those who died in the plague were twenty-four thousand. Then the Lord spoke to Moses, saying: "Phinehas the son of Eleazar, the son of Aaron the priest, has turned back My wrath from the children of Israel, because he was zealous with My zeal among them, so that I did not consume the children of Israel in My zeal."*

While we may feel disturbed by his response, the account of Phinehas exemplifies the zeal needed in the face of Israel's spiritual adultery and sexual immorality with their pagan neighbors. Fueled by zeal for God, Phinehas took a stand in demonstrating to the Israelite congregation that when God gives a command, it must be kept. Acting on the word of God, his initiative earns commendation, highlighting the importance of zealous obedience:

> **Psalm 106:28–31 (CJB)**
> *Now they joined themselves to Ba'al-P'or
> and ate meat sacrificed to dead things.*

> *Thus they provoked him to anger with their deeds,*
> *so that a plague broke out among them.*
> *Then Pinchas [Phinehas] stood up and executed judgment;*
> *so the plague was checked.*
> *That was credited to him as righteousness,*
> *through all generations forever.*

The zeal of Jesus, as seen in driving out the money changers from the temple, sets a powerful example. Motivated by godly zeal, Jesus took action to rectify disrespect toward God and the corruption that had set in among the temple authorities merchants, and money changers:

John 2:15-17
And He made a whip of cords, and drove them all out of the temple area, with the sheep and the oxen; and He poured out the coins of the money changers and overturned their tables; and to those who were selling the doves He said, "Take these things away from here; stop making My Father's house a place of business!" His disciples remembered that it was written: "Zeal for Your house will consume me."

When Jews from the diaspora traveled to go up to the temple, it was hard to bring animals for sacrifice due to the distance many of them were coming from. They had little choice but to purchase sacrificial animals there at the temple grounds. Merchants sold animals for sacrifice on the premises.

Additionally, since people were coming to Jerusalem from many nations bringing their own currencies with them, money changers provided the service of exchanging those currencies for local Roman coinage. The problem was that greed for profit ruled the day, and overcharging for animals and giving an unfair exchange rate became standard practice. Hence, Jesus' accusation in Mathew 21:13 that they had turned the temple court into a "den of robbers."

As seen in the examples set by Jesus and Phinehas that zeal, much like a cloak, is not just a passive covering; instead, it's an active force shaping the character of spiritual warriors, driving them to live out

The Cloak of Zeal

God's will with fervent dedication.

Zeal is the fuel that strengthens individuals to live according to God's way. Taking a stand for God's righteousness, serving our brothers and sisters in Christ through prayer and charitable actions, and seeking to serve others are all ways in which we demonstrate a zeal for the Father's house (think household).

Zeal can go awry if it's misplaced or misapplied. I'm reminded of a joke about misplaced zeal:

> A pastor, a Boy Scout, and a computer genius were the only passengers on a small plane. The pilot comes back to the cabin to report that the plane is going down, but there are only three parachutes.
>
> The pilot says, "I should have one because this is my plane and I have a wife and three small children." He takes a parachute and jumps.
>
> The computer genius says, "I should have one because I am the smartest man in the world. What would the world do without me?" He takes one and jumps.
>
> The pastor turns to the Boy Scout, and with a smile of resignation says, "You are young, and I have lived a rich life, so you take the parachute and I'll go down with the plane."
>
> The Boy Scout replied, "Relax, pastor; the smartest man in the world just picked up my backpack and jumped out."

All of them had zeal to live, but one didn't have right knowledge!

Speaking of those among the Jewish people who had rejected Jesus as Messiah, Paul wrote in Romans 10:2: "For I bear them witness that they have a zeal for God, but not according to knowledge."

As "a Pharisee of Pharisees," Paul was zealous in persecuting the messianic community (Philippians 3:6), until he learned the stunning truth that wasn't what God wanted. Once he was confronted by the very LORD he was persecuting and came to the understanding that Yeshua was indeed the promised Messiah, he put his new knowledge to use, zealously spreading the message of redemption.

When I was Mormon I had zeal for spreading the Mormon gospel. At Christmas time I gave Books of Mormon to the mailman, to neighbors, and to my husband's piano students (along with homemade cookies).

Sometimes, because we were musicians, we would be invited to sing for special programs at local Christian churches and we always chose songs with lyrics that expressed Mormon doctrine or we would alter the wording of Christian songs to reflect LDS teachings.

My kids were zealous for Mormonism too. There was a candy store in our neighborhood that my kids used to walk to for treats. One time the store was vandalized and my 11-year-old son and his friend went there with brooms to help the owner clean up. The owner was surprised that these two young kids had offered to help. My son explained with pride, "We're helping because we're Mormons!"

We had great zeal as members of the LDS community, but it was based on wrong knowledge. That also serves as a lesson for Christians to be discerning. I don't know what these church leaders were thinking by inviting us—practitioners and promoters of a false gospel—to sing in their worship services!

After leaving Mormonism for Biblical faith, I had a different kind of zeal, which was good, except for one thing; it was a zeal without tact. Sir Isaac Newton said this:

> *Tact is the art of making a point without making an enemy.*

From my book, *Confessions of an Ex-Mormon*:

> I couldn't stop telling people why Mormonism wasn't true whether they wanted to know or not, whether they were interested or not, or whether they were Mormons or not. No one was exempt from hearing about it, not even people on the street.

The Cloak of Zeal

One time as I was driving down a major road in North Las Vegas, I saw two LDS missionaries talking to a guy wearing a sandwich board advertising something at the corner of an intersection. I could see that they handed him what looked like a Book of Mormon.

Naturally I thought it was a great opportunity to set things straight, so I made a U-turn (legally, of course) and drove back to the parking lot close to the guy and waited until the missionaries got on their bicycles and pedaled away. There was landscaping between me and him, so I leapt over a few bushes, climbed over a short retaining wall, swept my disheveled hair from my face, and approached the man.

"Hello!" I greeted warmly. "How are you? I noticed two Mormon missionaries talking to you. Are you LDS?" He said he wasn't, so I continued. "Well, I used to be Mormon. I was LDS for 26 years and I just found out that the Church isn't true and that the Book of Mormon is a fraud. I just wanted to give you something to read that shows the other side."

At this I whipped out a copy of my exit-story (testimony of leaving Mormonism), which I had printed out and made into a booklet at Office Depot. I carried stacks of them in my vehicle wherever I went, just for occasions like this. The man thanked me and I left feeling happy that I may have prevented another spiritual casualty. (Tennant, Confessions of an Ex-Mormon: What I Wish I Knew When I Left the Church, 33–35.).[2]

On another occasion, I knew that my best friend, who was LDS, had

---

2. Tennant, Tracy. Confessions of an Ex-Mormon: What I Wish I Knew When I Left the Church. From Kolob to Calvary, 2017.

invited a non-member over to share the Mormon gospel with him. So I drove over there and slipped my testimony booklet into the front seat of the man's car through his open window. I'll just say this; after a few more of these kinds of episodes, I no longer had a best friend.

> There's a big problem in relationships, religion aside, and it's basically talking too much and listening too little. We want so desperately for our own views to be heard and understood, that we often forget that other people feel the same way and have the same needs to be heard and understood.
>
> **Proverbs 18:2**
> *A fool takes no pleasure in trying to understand; he only wants to express his own opinion.*
>
> *Proverbs 18:13*
> *To answer someone before hearing him out is both stupid and embarrassing.*
>
> You can't argue someone into the kingdom of heaven. Getting into endless arguments over which view is right is fruitless, and harms the most important relationships you have: marital and parental [familial, and of course, evangelistic]. Mutual love and respect go far in preparing hearts to listen. (Ibid., 35)

There's a saying that goes like this: "A man convinced against his will is of the same opinion still." Recall Ephesians 6:15; "and having strapped on your feet the preparation of the gospel of peace," not the gospel of antagonism. If a person takes offense, let the offense be because of the gospel message, not because of your conduct.

Jesus and Phinehas both encountered situations that showed disrespect for God, and they took appropriate action. While we aren't to run anyone through with a spear or overturn tables at religious venues, we should be driven to take a stand for God's ways when we see them being defiled or desecrated. The most effective way to do that is by letting our words and deeds uphold truth.

Zeal should be a transformative force that causes us to examine ourselves and our motives and give us a fervent desire to eliminate sin from our own lives. It's not just an outward display, but a powerful inward motivation to purify ourselves as temples of the Holy Spirit, purchased at a high price by Jesus' sacrifice. Godly sorrow leading to repentance is something that springs out of a healthy zeal for the Lord as we recognize the holiness of His indwelling Spirit.

Furthermore, our zeal for the Lord should extend to a passionate concern for fellow believers, especially the remnant, reflecting the example of a Epaphras:

> **Colossians 4:12-13**
> *Epaphras, who is one of you, a bondservant of Christ, greets you, always laboring fervently for you in prayers, that you may stand perfect and complete in all the will of God. For I bear him witness that **he has a great zeal for you**, and those who are in Laodicea, and those in Hierapolis* [Emphasis mine].

A true disciple of Christ is driven by zeal for the well-being of others out of a general genuine passion for the Father's household. The apostle Paul is a wonderful example of someone zealous not only for God, but for his fellowman. Likewise, those in the messianic community in turn were zealous for their beloved Rabbi Paul:

> **2 Corinthians 7:2–13**
> *Make room in your hearts for us. We have wronged no one, we have corrupted no one, we have taken advantage of no one. I do not say this to condemn you, for I said before that you are in our hearts, to die together and to live together. I am acting with great boldness toward you; I have great pride in you; I am filled with comfort. In all our affliction, I am overflowing with joy.*
>
> *For even when we came into Macedonia, our bodies had no rest, but we were afflicted at every turn—fighting without and fear*

within. But God, who comforts the downcast, comforted us by the coming of Titus, and not only by his coming but also by the comfort with which he was comforted by you, as he told us of your longing, your mourning, your zeal for me, so that I rejoiced still more.

For even if I made you grieve with my letter, I do not regret it—though I did regret it, for I see that that letter grieved you, though only for a while. As it is, I rejoice, not because you were grieved, but because you were grieved into repenting. For you felt a godly grief, so that you suffered no loss through us.

For godly grief produces a repentance that leads to salvation without regret, whereas worldly grief produces death. For see what earnestness this godly grief has produced in you, but also what eagerness to clear yourselves, what indignation, what fear, what longing, what zeal, what punishment! At every point you have proved yourselves innocent in the matter.

So although I wrote to you, it was not for the sake of the one who did the wrong, nor for the sake of the one who suffered the wrong, but in order that your earnestness for us might be revealed to you in the sight of God. Therefore we are comforted.

Revelation 3:15–16, 19 is a sobering chastisement of those who are not zealous for God. Jesus said to the assembly at Laodicea:

*I know your deeds, that you are neither cold nor hot; I wish that you were cold or hot. So because you are lukewarm, and neither hot nor cold, I will spit you out of My mouth. Those whom I love, I reprove and discipline; therefore **be zealous** and repent.*

When our zeal is worn as a cloak, it will provide warmth, comfort, and defense against the storms Satan sends to discourage us and destroy our morale. It will also propel us into action—standing firm against the onslaught of evil we face in these perilous times.

11

The Spear of Prayer

*With every prayer and request, pray at all times in the Spirit,
and with this in view, be alert with all perseverance
and every request for all the saints
Ephesians 6:18*

In his book *Dressed to Kill: A Biblical Approach to Spiritual Warfare and Armor*, Rick Renner calls this last piece of weaponry the "lance of prayer and supplication" ("lance," as used in a jousting tournament). He writes:

> When you wield the lance of prayer and supplication, this powerful tool is thrust forward into the spirit realm against the malevolent forces of the adversary. By forcibly hurling this divine instrument into the face of the enemy, you exercise the power God has given you to stop major obstacles from developing in your personal life (Renner, 2013).[1]

---

1. Rick Renner, Dressed to Kill: A Biblical Approach to Spiritual Warfare and Armor (Harrison House, 2013), 434

Theologian Albert Barnes in the 1800s, wrote,

> No matter how complete the armor; no matter how skilled we may be in the science of war; no matter how courageous we may be, we may be certain that without prayer we shall be defeated. God alone can give the victory; and when the Christian soldier goes forth armed completely for the spiritual conflict, if he looks to God by prayer, he may be sure of a triumph. This prayer is not to be intermittent. It is to be always. In every temptation and spiritual conflict we are to pray.

> With all prayer and supplication - With all kinds of prayer; prayer in the closet, the family, the social meeting, the great assembly; prayer at the usual hours, prayer when we are specially tempted, and when we feel just like praying (see the notes, Matthew 6:6) prayer in the form of supplication for ourselves, and in the form of intercession for others. This is, after all, the great weapon of our spiritual armor, and by this we may hope to prevail (Barnes, n.d.)[2]

We must be unwavering in our commitment to prayer if we are to keep a continual open line of connection with our Heavenly Father. This is what it means to be equipped in God's armor. As Captain of the Lord's Host, only He knows how to bring about victory, and we need to be ready and able to discern His voice.

As former combat marine Jamie Walden and U.S. Army retired chaplain Colonel David Giammona would tell you, comms—or communications—is vital in wartime. In regard to communication in the various branches of the military, it plays a critical role in day-to-day operations, enabling commanders to efficiently guide their troops,

---

[2]. "Ephesians 6 Commentary - Albert Barnes' Notes on the Whole Bible," Truth According to Scripture, n.d., https://www.truthaccordingtoscripture.com/commentaries/bnb/ephesians-6.php.

transmit orders, and coordinate diverse units. In the absence of effective communication, military endeavors can swiftly deteriorate, resulting in disarray, confusion, and ultimate failure.

A primary function of military communication is the transmission of orders and instructions to the units. These instructions can be basic maneuvers to intricate operations that demand coordination between the various teams. Military communication systems have to be secure so that enemies cannot intercept and know of the plans that are soon to be carried out. The information transmitted to the units must be trustworthy and reliable. Incorrect information, disinformation, and propaganda leads not only to failure, but ultimately costs lives. Methods of communication need to be cutting-edge and able to disseminate information and orders quickly. Unnecessary delays can again result in catastrophe.

Another vital aspect of reliable communication systems is gathering and disseminating intelligence. Troops need to know where enemy forces are and the strategies they intend to employ. Reconnaissance missions give leaders the information they need to effectively manage and instruct the combat units they oversee.

I think of Joshua and Caleb being sent out with ten other men to reconnoiter Canaanite territory, as described in Numbers chapters 13 and 14. They were instructed by Moses:

> **Numbers 13:13–17**
> *Go up there into the Negev; then go up into the hill country. See what the land is like, and whether the people who live in it are strong or weak, whether they are few or many. And how is the land in which they live, is it good or bad? And how are the cities in which they live, are the people in open camps or in fortifications? And how is the land, is it productive or unproductive? Are there trees in it or not? And show yourselves courageous and get some of the fruit of the land.*

The significance of effective communication in military operations should not be taken lightly. It's easy to see the parallels between military comms and spiritual warfare comms. Our greatest asset in life, spiritual growth, and spiritual warfare is prayer. Prayer is not only a great defense, but an effective offensive weapon as well, as illustrated by Rick Renner's description of it as the "lance of prayer," or what I prefer to call the spear of prayer.

James 5:16–18
A prayer of a righteous person, when it is brought about, can accomplish much. Elijah was a man with a nature like ours, and he prayed earnestly that it would not rain, and it did not rain on the earth for three years and six months. Then he prayed again, and the sky poured rain and the earth produced its fruit.

I love the account of Elisha when Aram planned to attack Israel because it illustrates what effective field communications between the Kingdom Warrior and God can do:

2 Kings 6:8–20 (CJB)
Now the king of Aram went to war against Isra'el; and in consulting his servants he said, "I'll set up my ambush camp in such-and-such a place." The man of God sent this message to the king of Isra'el: "Be careful not to go past such-and-such a place, because Aram will attack there." So the king of Isra'el sent men to the place the man of God had told him and warned him about, and he took special precautions there.

This happened more than once or twice, and it greatly upset the king of Aram. He called his servants and said to them, "Tell me which of you is betraying us to the king of Isra'el?" [Who's leaking intel?]

One of his servants replied, "It's not that, my lord, king. Rather, Elisha, the prophet who is in Isra'el, tells the king of Isra'el the words you speak privately in your own bedroom!" He said, "Go and see where he is, so that I can send and bring him here." They told him, "He's in Dotan."

The Spear of Prayer

So he sent horses, chariots and a large army there; they came by night and surrounded the city. The servant of the man of God got up early in the morning; on going outside, he saw an army with horses and chariots surrounding the city. His servant said to him, "Oh, my master, this is terrible! What are we going to do?" He answered, "Don't be afraid — those who are with us outnumber those who are with them!"

Elisha prayed, "Adonai, I ask you to open his eyes, so that he can see." Then Adonai opened the young man's eyes, and he saw: there before him, all around Elisha, the mountain was covered with horses and fiery chariots.

When they came down to him, Elisha prayed to Adonai, "Please strike these people blind"; and he struck them blind, as Elisha had asked. Next, Elisha told them, "You've lost your way, and this isn't even the right city. Follow me, and I'll take you to the man you're looking for." Then he led them to Shomron. On their arrival in Shomron, Elisha said, "Adonai, open the eyes of these men, so that they can see." Adonai opened their eyes, and they saw: there they were, in the middle of Shomron.

Note that it wasn't physical blindness, like their eyes stopped working. It was more like in the first *Star Wars* movie when the Stormtroopers stopped Luke Skywalker and Jedi Master Obi-Wan Kenobi:

Stormtrooper: *Let me see your identification.*
Obi-Wan: *You don't need to see his identification.*
Stormtrooper: *We don't need to see his identification.*
Obi-Wan: *These aren't the droids you're looking for.*
Stormtrooper: *These aren't the droids we're looking for.*
Obi-Wan: *He can go about his business.*
Stormtrooper: *You can go about your business.*
Obi-Wan: *Move along.*
Stormtrooper: *Move along, move along.*

2 Kings 6:21–23
When they had come into Samaria, Elisha said, "Lord, open the eyes of these men, so that they may see." So the Lord opened their eyes, and they saw; and behold, they were in the midst of Samaria.

Then the king of Israel when he saw them, said to Elisha, "My father, shall I kill them? Shall I kill them?"

But he answered, "You shall not kill them. Would you kill those whom you have taken captive with your sword and your bow? Set bread and water before them, so that they may eat and drink, and go to their master."

So he provided a large feast for them; and when they had eaten and drunk, he sent them away, and they went to their master. And the marauding bands of Arameans did not come again into the land of Israel.

God is merciful, as well as just! A strong prayer life brings direction and instruction from the Lord. He is ready and willing to answer our prayers. We might not like the answer—for instance, it might be "No" or "Not yet," but we can rest assured that our Father knows best. And when it seems like God is silent, it's possible He wants you to wait patiently for the answer while trusting that He hears you and is not ignoring you. Regardless of the timing of the answers, we are to pray always. Jesus gives us an example of what it means to pray at all times:

Luke 18:1–8
Now He was telling them a parable to show that at all times they ought to pray and not become discouraged, saying, "In a certain city there was a judge who did not fear God and did not respect any person. Now there was a widow in that city, and she kept coming to him, saying, 'Give me justice against my opponent.'

For a while he was unwilling; but later he said to himself, 'Even though I do not fear God nor respect any person, yet because this widow is bothering me, I will give her justice; otherwise by continually coming she will wear me out.'"

And the Lord said, "Listen to what the unrighteous judge said; now, will God not bring about justice for His elect who cry out to Him day and night, and will He delay long for them? I tell you that He will bring about justice for them quickly. However, when the Son of Man comes, will He find faith on the earth?"

This widow remained persistent with dogged determination to see that she received justice. She never gave up. "Praying always" doesn't mean that every waking moment we need to be engaged in conversing with the Lord. It means cultivating a connection to our Father in Heaven that's maintained by praying regularly and often. Studying and internalizing His written word, as well as godly living will allow us to come before His throne with confidence on every occasion and in a day of need or distress.

The apostle Paul encourages us to pray:

Philippians 4:6
Do not be anxious about anything, but in everything by prayer and pleading with thanksgiving let your requests be made known to God.

When wielding the spear of prayer, we are told to pray at all times in the Spirit. Some people have interpreted this to mean praying in tongues. What a blessing it is to have a special prayer language! But for those who don't have one, does that mean they cannot pray effectively? *GotQuestions.org* answers this question:

Praying in the Spirit is mentioned three times in Scripture:

1 Corinthians 14:15
So what shall I do? I will pray with my spirit, but I will also

pray with my mind; I will sing with my spirit, but I will also sing with my mind."

Ephesians 6:18
And pray in the Spirit on all occasions with all kinds of prayers and requests. With this in mind, be alert and always keep on praying for all the saints.

Jude v. 20
But you, dear friends, build yourselves up in your most holy faith and pray in the Holy Spirit.

The Greek word translated "pray in" can have several different meanings. It can mean "by means of," "with the help of," "in the sphere of," and "in connection to." Praying in the Spirit does not refer to the words we are saying. Rather, it refers to how we are praying. Praying in the Spirit is praying according to the Spirit's leading. It is praying for things the Spirit leads us to pray for.

Some, based on 1 Corinthians 14:15, equate praying in the Spirit with praying in tongues. Discussing the gift of tongues, Paul mentions "pray with my spirit." 1 Corinthians 14:14 states that when a person prays in tongues, he does not know what he is saying, since it is spoken in a language he does not know. Further, no one else can understand what is being said, unless there is an interpreter (1 Corinthians 14:27-28).

In Ephesians 6:18, Paul instructs us to "pray in the Spirit on all occasions with all kinds of prayers and requests." How are we to pray with all kinds of prayers and requests and pray for the saints, if no one, including the person praying, understands what is being said?

Therefore, praying in the Spirit should be understood

as praying in the power of the Spirit, by the leading of the Spirit, and according to His will, not as praying in tongues (GotQuestions.org, n.d.).[3]

The Holy Spirit has a huge role in the prayers of believers:

Romans 8:26-27
Likewise the Spirit also helps in our weaknesses. For we do not know what we should pray for as we ought, but the Spirit [itself] makes intercession for us with groanings which cannot be uttered. Now He who searches the hearts knows what the mind of the Spirit is, because [it] makes intercession for the saints according to the will of God.

Since we don't always know how to pray as we should, if we have the Spirit in us and are led by that same Spirit, Paul says the Holy Spirit will make intercession for us. This means that even when we don't know how to pray or what we should be praying for in certain situations, God knows our hearts desires, and we have the Holy Spirit to intercede for us.

Who and what should we be praying for? Study the epistles written by Paul. Each one typically begins with praises and honor to God and His goodness. He often starts with expressions of gratitude for that particular church body. He typically ends with instructions, concerns, and specific prayer requests.

◊ **Pray for Specific People.**

Romans 16:1–16 and verses 21–23 is dedicated to greeting various individuals whom Paul commends for their love and service in the kingdom. Likewise, in our prayer we can lift up the names of people we care about, giving thanks to God for them and asking His provision and care for them.

---

3. "What is praying in the spirit?," Got Questions Ministries, accessed February 28, 2024, https://www.gotquestions.org/praying-Spirit.html

◊ **Pray for discernment and alertness.**

In **Romans 16:17–18**, Paul is concerned about people who come into the congregation to cause dissension, and who use flattery to deceive the church body and lead them astray.

1 Corinthians 16:14
Be on the alert, stand firm in the faith, act like men, be strong. Let all that you do be done in love.

◊ **Pray for wisdom and understanding.**

Romans 16:19 is Paul's admonition "to be wise in what is good and innocent in what is evil."

Colossians 1:1–10
For this reason also, since the day we heard of it, we have not ceased to pray for you and to ask that you may be filled with the knowledge of His will in all spiritual wisdom and understanding, so that you will walk in a manner worthy of the Lord, to please Him in all respects, bearing fruit in every good work and increasing in the knowledge of God;

◊ **Pray for spiritual gifts to enrich your local fellowship.**

1 Corinthians 1:4–9
I thank my God always concerning you for the grace of God which was given you in Christ Jesus, that in everything you were enriched in Him, in all speech and all knowledge, even as the testimony concerning Christ was confirmed in you, so that you are not lacking in any gift, awaiting eagerly the revelation of our Lord Jesus Christ, who will also confirm you to the end, blameless in the day of our Lord Jesus Christ. God is faithful, through whom you were called into fellowship with His Son, Jesus Christ our Lord.

◊ **Pray for unity and peace among believers.**

1 Corinthians 1:10
Now I exhort you, brethren, by the name of our Lord Jesus Christ, that you all agree and that there be no divisions among you, but that you be made complete in the same mind and in the same judgment.

2 Corinthians 13:11
Finally, brethren, rejoice, be made complete, be comforted, be like-minded, live in peace; and the God of love and peace will be with you.

◊ **Pray for the comfort of those afflicted and suffering.**

2 Corinthians 1:3–4
Blessed be the God and Father of our Lord Jesus Christ, the Father of mercies and God of all comfort, who comforts us in all our affliction so that we will be able to comfort those who are in any affliction with the comfort with which we ourselves are comforted by God.

◊ **Pray for self-awareness and for help in doing right.**

2 Corinthians 13:5–7
Test yourselves to see if you are in the faith; examine yourselves! Or do you not recognize this about yourselves, that Jesus Christ is in you—unless indeed you fail the test? But I trust that you will realize that we ourselves do not fail the test. Now we pray to God that you do no wrong; not that we ourselves may appear approved, but that you may do what is right, even though we may appear unapproved.

Galatians 6:9
Let us not lose heart in doing good, for in due time we will reap if we do not grow weary. So then, while we have opportunity, let

us do good to all people, and especially to those who are of the household of the faith.

◊ **Pray for provision.**

Philippians 4:19
And my God will supply all your needs according to His riches in glory in Christ Jesus.

◊ **Pray for all the saints for everything.**

Ephesians 6:18–19
With all prayer and petition pray at all times in the Spirit, and with this in view, be on the alert with all perseverance and petition for all the saints, and pray on my behalf, that utterance may be given to me in the opening of my mouth, to make known with boldness the mystery of the gospel.

1 Thessalonians 1:2–3
We give thanks to God always for all of you, making mention of you in our prayers; constantly bearing in mind your work of faith and labor of love and steadfastness of hope in our Lord Jesus Christ in the presence of our God and Father.

◊ **Pray for missionaries and the spreading of the gospel.**

Colossians 4:2–6
Devote yourselves to prayer, keeping alert in it with an attitude of thanksgiving; praying at the same time for us as well, that God will open up to us a door for the word, so that we may speak forth the mystery of Christ, for which I have also been imprisoned; that I may make it clear in the way I ought to speak. Conduct yourselves with wisdom toward outsiders, making the most of the opportunity. Let your speech always be with grace, as though seasoned with salt, so that you will know how you should respond to each person.

◊ **Pray for your sanctification.**

1 Thessalonians 5:23
Now may the God of peace Himself sanctify you entirely; and may your spirit and soul and body be preserved complete, without blame at the coming of our Lord Jesus Christ.

Paul Praises and Gives Thanks to God.

- Blessed be the God and Father of our Lord Jesus Christ…
- Blessed be the God and Father of our Lord Jesus Christ, who has blessed us with every spiritual blessing…
- We give thanks to God, the Father of our Lord Jesus Christ…
- We give thanks to God always for all of you…
- I thank Christ Jesus our Lord, who has strengthened me…

Paul Shows Love for the Community of Faith.

Paul gives us a great pattern to follow. Although not all the verses listed are directly about prayer, but they give us an idea of what we can pray for and about. In telling the various messianic communities to greet certain individuals, he is giving them a list of persons he cares deeply about.

He also gives details about those whom he names, and demonstrates that we should give thanks to God for all the people we care for. See how he rejoices over those he ministers with, calling them:

- A servant of the church.
- My fellow workers in Christ Jesus.
- My kinsmen and my fellow prisoners.
- My beloved.
- The approved in Christ.
- A choice man.
- My true child in the faith.
- My beloved brethren…my joy and crown.

Paul Warns and Instructs.

- Keep your eye on those who cause dissensions and hindrances, and turn away from them (Romans 16:17).
- (Those who cause dissensions) deceive the hearts of the unsuspecting (Romans 16:18).
- Be wise in what is good, and innocent in what is evil (Romans 16:19).
- Do all things without grumbling or disputing (Philippians 2:14).
- Be on the alert, stand firm in the faith, act like men (and women), be strong (1 Corinthians 16:13).
- Let all that you do be done in love (1 Corinthians 16:14).
- Test yourselves to see if you are in the faith; examine yourselves (2 Corinthians 13:5).
- Rejoice, be made complete, be comforted, be like-minded, live in peace (2 Corinthians 13:11).
- Don't lose heart in doing good; do good to all people, especially to those in the faith (Galatians 6:1–11).
- Devote yourselves to prayer, keeping alert in it with an attitude of thanksgiving (Colossians 4:2).
- Conduct yourselves with wisdom toward outsiders, making the most of the opportunity (Colossians 4:5).
- Let your speech always be with grace so you'll know how to respond to each person (Colossians 4:6).
- With all prayer and petition pray at all times in the Spirit (Ephesians 6:18).

These are all things we can pray about! "Lord, help me recognize and avoid dissensions that hinder others in their walk. I pray for discernment so that I'm not deceived. Help me be wise. Help me live in peace. Lead me in doing good to all people..." You get the picture.

Paul Prays for Others.

- Pray that God will supply all your needs (Philippians 4:19).
- May the God of peace Himself sanctify you entirely (1

Thessalonians 5:23a).
- May your spirit and soul and body be preserved complete, without blame (1 Thessalonians 5:23b).
- Pray that you'll filled with the knowledge of His will in all spiritual wisdom and understanding (Colossians 1:9).
- Pray you'll walk in a manner worthy of the Lord, to please Him in all respects, bearing fruit in every good work and increasing in the knowledge of God (Colossians 1:10).
- Pray to be strengthened with all power, according to His glorious might, for the attaining of all steadfastness and patience (Colossians 1:11).
- May the Lord cause you to increase and abound in love for one another, and for all people (1 Thessalonians 3:12).
- I pray that the eyes of your heart may be enlightened, so that you will know what is the hope of His calling, what are the riches of the glory of His inheritance in the saints (Ephesians 1:18).

Praying for our needs and the needs of others develops godly qualities within and brings blessings without.

Paul Makes Prayer Requests.

- Pray on my behalf, that utterance may be given to me in the opening of my mouth (Ephesians 6:19).
- Pray that I'll be bold (Ephesians 6:20).
- Pray for us that the word of the Lord will spread rapidly and be glorified (2 Thessalonians 3:1).
- That we will be rescued from perverse and evil men (2 Thessalonians 3:2).
- Pray that I may be rescued from those who are disobedient in Judea, that my service for Jerusalem may prove acceptable to the saints, that I may come to you in joy by the will of God and find refreshing rest in your company (Romans 15:30–32).

We can pray for guidance when to speak, what to say, and when to be silent. We pray for protection. We pray for times of rest and refreshing.

Our leaders and others who serve in ministry need our prayers, We mustn't forget them. They have heavy loads to carry as they tend to the needs of their congregations and followers in person and online. Demands are put upon their time even while they have families of their own. They sometimes (and maybe more often than they let on) suffer from exhaustion, discouragement, sickness, and financial lack.

Beyond praying for ourselves and those we know, it's imperative to pray for believers around the world whom we *don't* know! According to *OpenDoors.org*, updated for 2024, "more than 365 million Christians suffer high levels of persecution and discrimination for their faith."[4] These precious men, women, and children face danger daily, and they need our prayers so heaven will move on their behalf.

Jesus Gave a Pattern for Prayer.

> **Luke 11:1 (CJB)**
> *It happened that while Jesus was praying in a certain place, after He had finished, one of His disciples said to Him, "Lord, teach us to pray just as John also taught his disciples."*

Of course, being devout Jewish men, the disciples knew how to pray—it was a part of their lives since their youth. In Bible times, those who wanted to study Torah deeply would attach themselves to a sage or rabbi and become his disciples—students. These teachers would craft a short liturgical prayer for their particular school of discipleship. This special prayer would be in addition to the traditional daily prayers, petitions, and blessings.

The disciples of Jesus wanted Him to teach them their own special or unique prayer:

> **Matthew 6:9-13 (CJB)**
> *Our Father in heaven!*
> *May your Name be kept holy.*

---

4. "World Watchlist 2024." Open Doors/Persecution/Countries/. Open Doors, Accessed January 30, 2024. https://www.opendoors.org/en-US/persecution/countries/

The Spear of Prayer

May your Kingdom come,
your will be done on earth as in heaven.
Give us the food we need today.
Forgive us what we have done wrong,
as we too have forgiven those who have wronged us.
And do not lead us into hard testing,
but keep us safe from the Evil One.
For kingship, power and glory are yours forever.

Jesus forewarned us about the time we now live in—the end of the age, and instructed us to pray always so we will have the strength to make it through:

Luke 21:34–36 (CJB)
But keep watch on yourselves, or your hearts will become dulled by carousing, drunkenness and the worries of everyday living, and that Day will be sprung upon you suddenly like a trap! For it will close in on everyone, no matter where they live, throughout the whole world. Stay alert, always praying that you will have the strength to escape all the things that will happen and to stand in the presence of the Son of Man.

Just as a spear has multiple uses, prayer also is multifaceted and effective in our daily walk with the Lord. It's so important to understand and be mindful of the nature of prayer because it's a gateway to the supernatural. Prayer is a portal that accesses the throne of God directly. It's also a great privilege, and one that shouldn't be taken lightly.

It's true that prayer changes things and that there's power in prayer. But prayer in and of itself is not a mystical force that anyone can apply like a charm or incantation. Heavens no! Prayer is a channel of communication between heaven and earth—between us and the Creator of the universe. At its core, prayer is fellowship, a direct line of communication with our Father in Heaven. Yeshua, our King and High Priest is what makes prayer so powerful. Once we grasp this concept, prayer becomes a mighty spiritual weapon of warfare that moves mountains and pierces the darkness!

12

The Walk of a Warrior

For we are His workmanship, created in Christ Jesus for good works, which God prepared beforehand so that we would walk in them.
Ephesians 2:10

The warrior's walk is one of circumspection, soberness, and diligence considering the time in which we live. Holiness doesn't mean we all march in uniformity, living a life of strict asceticism. There is freedom in the kingdom of God—not freedom to sin, but freedom to serve the Lord—not out of compulsion, but out of love and devotion.

> **Galatians 5:1, 4–6 (CJB)**
> *You who are trying to be declared righteous by God through legalism have severed yourselves from the Messiah! You have fallen away from God's grace! For it is by the power of the Spirit, who works in us because we trust and are faithful, that we confidently expect our hope of attaining righteousness to be fulfilled. When we are united with the Messiah Yeshua, neither being circumcised nor being uncircumcised matters; what matters is trusting faithfulness expressing itself through love.*

What matters is "circumcision of the heart," a symbolic cutting away of the flesh (worldliness and self-seeking) and a reminder to us that we belong to the Creator of the universe.

> Practically, we can't show the world we've been circumcised, but God's covenant extends further than just the physical realm. A way has been provided in which our words and actions can show the nations God has touched us. We read His promise in Deuteronomy 30:6:

> *"Moreover, the Lord your God will circumcise your heart and the heart of your descendants, to love the Lord your God with all your heart and with all your soul, in order that you may live."*

> This type of circumcision, by definition a circumcision of the spirit and not the flesh, goes to the heart of a man, to his soul, his essence, his attitudes and relationship with God. Because this theme of an inner circumcision is so important, God repeats and stresses it, as in Deuteronomy 10:12-16:

> *"And now, Israel, what does the Lord your God require from you, but to fear the Lord your God, to walk in all His ways and love Him, and to serve the Lord your God with all your heart and with all your soul.* ***And to keep the Lord's commandments and His statutes which I am commanding you today for your good?***

> ...Over and over again God probes the inner man, the real person. His discerning eyes won't allow us to hide behind social facades, adopted mannerisms or walls of materialism. Before God each man is seen just as he is. His innermost thoughts, thoughts he may wish to

hide from the world, are exposed by the light of God (Friedman, 1981).[1]

It's important to understand that God expects us to keep His commandments, not for salvation—Jesus took upon *Himself* the penalty for our sins. But isn't obedience a testimony to the fact that we are saved? We're saved from destruction, saved from the penalty our sin demands, saved to operate as citizens of heaven, saved for the kingdom of God to dwell with Him forever. What does Scripture say?

> **James 2:18–19**
> *But someone may well say, "You have faith and I have works; show me your faith without the works, and I will show you my faith by my works." You believe that God is one. You do well; the demons also believe, and shudder. But are you willing to acknowledge, you foolish person, that faith without works is useless?*

> **Ephesians 2:8–9**
> *For by grace you have been saved through faith; and this is not of yourselves, it is the gift of God; not a result of works, so that no one may boast. For we are His workmanship, created in Christ Jesus for good works, which God prepared beforehand so that we would walk in them.*

Although ultimately God is the Surgeon who circumcises our hearts, we have a role as well. We partner with Him in that procedure by the choices we make on a daily basis. In every circumstance we can choose right or wrong, good or bad, love and kindness or anger and hate, godly speech or vulgarity. We carry some responsibility for the way we live as children of the Most High. We ought to pray as David did:

---

1. Robert Friedman, "Circumcision of the Heart: Exploring Moses' Odd Metaphor for Israel's Relationship to God.," Jews for Jesus, March 1, 1981, accessed February 26, 2024, https://jewsforjesus.org/learn/circumcision-of-the-heart.

Psalm 51:10–12 (NLT)
Create in me a clean heart, O God.
Renew a loyal spirit within me.
Do not banish me from your presence,
and don't take your Holy Spirit from me.
Restore to me the joy of your salvation,
and make me willing to obey you.

If you bristle at the thought of needing to keep the commandments, perhaps it's a good moment to pause and examine your heart. Again, we're not talking about keeping the commandments to be saved; we're talking about keeping the commandments to "put our money where our mouth is." If we don't demonstrate our faith by our works, we're doing nothing more than giving lip service to God. So what commandments are we referring to? Jesus encapsulated them all into two things:

Mark 12:28–31
One of the teachers of religious law was standing there listening to the debate. He realized that Jesus had answered well, so he asked, "Of all the commandments, which is the most important?" Jesus replied, "The most important commandment is this: 'Listen, O Israel! The Lord our God is the one and only Lord. And you must love the Lord your God with all your heart, all your soul, all your mind, and all your strength.' The second is equally important: 'Love your neighbor as yourself.' No other commandment is greater than these."

Righteousness is the most effective weapon there is against the Enemy, and we are clothed with the righteousness of our Lord and Savior Jesus Christ! Satan and the fallen were defeated at Calvary, it's just that they haven't yet surrendered. They embrace a "scorched earth policy" as a military strategy. They already know they are doomed to the *Lake of Fire*, so their goal is to take as many people with them as possible. In their twisted view, if *they* can't have the planet, then neither can God's human family.

How do we fight against a formidable enemy like that? We get off

The Walk of a Warrior

the bench and run onto the field. We stop being spectators and start being spiritual quarterbacks. Every soul we recruit for Team Kingdom, a touchdown is scored. Every evil we tackle, is one less player on Team Darkness. We hit forcefully and strategically to take down the opposing team. If we are not "all in," we'll be trampled. And when we get knocked down, we get back up, dust ourselves off, and regroup with our teammates.

In this deadly game we've been commissioned to play, we need every blood-bought believer engaged. We need running backs, line backers, coaches, referees, and cheerleaders. Every one of us has an assignment, individually designed according to the unique qualities and giftings the Holy Spirit bestows upon us. No one has the luxury of being spectators sitting in the stands. This "game" isn't played for entertainment; it's played for keeps. Winner takes all. So suit up in your spiritual gear and run to the battle. The victory is ours!

He has told you,
O man, what is good;
And what does the Lord
require of you
But to do justice,
to love kindness,
And to walk humbly
with your God?

Micah 6:8

Bibliography

Azlyrics.biz. "Gilbert and Sullivan – This Helmet, I Suppose Lyrics," n.d. https://azlyrics.biz/g/gilbert-and-sullivan-lyrics/gilbert-and-sullivan-this-helmet-i-suppose-lyrics/.

Biblehub.com. "Ephesians 6:11 Commentaries: Put on the Full Armorof God, so That You Will Be Able to Stand Firm Against the Schemes of the Devil.," n.d. https://biblehub.com/commentaries/ephesians/6-11.htm.

Bible Study Tools. "Hetoimazo Meaning - Greek Lexicon - New Testament (NAS)," n.d. https://www.biblestudytools.com/lexicons/greek/nas/hetoimazo.html.

Bolinger, Hope. "What Is the Sword of the Spirit and How Should I Use It?" *Crosswalk.com*, March 25, 2022. https://www.crosswalk.com/faith/bible-study/what-is-the-sword-of-the-spirit-and-how-should-i-use-it.html.

Brand, Miryam. "The Benei Elohim, the Watchers, and the Origins of Evil." *The Torah — Com.* Accessed February 26, 2024. https://www.thetorah.com/article/the-benei-elohim-the-watchers-and-the-origins-of-evil.

Dart, John. "Mormons Modify Temple Rites: Ceremony: Woman's Vow to Obey Husband Is Dropped. Changes Are Called Most Significant since 1978." *Los Angeles Times*. 1990.

Dupont. "What Is Kevlar®?," n.d. https://www.dupont.com/what-is-kevlar.html.

Friedman, Robert. "Circumcision of the Heart: Exploring Moses' Odd Metaphor for Israel's Relationship to God." *Jews for Jesus*, March 1, 1981. Accessed February 26, 2024. https://jewsforjesus.org/learn/circumcision-of-the-heart.

Gateway, Tolkien. "Mithril - Tolkien Gateway." *Tolkien Gateway*, January 13, 2023. https://tolkiengateway.net/wiki/Mithril.

GotQuestions.org. "Helmet of Salvation," January 4, 2022. https://www.gotquestions.org/helmet-of-salvation.html.

GotQuestions.org. "Praying in the Spirit," January 4, 2022. https://www.gotquestions.org/praying-Spirit.html.

Logos Sermons. "Are You God' Wife?," February 13, 2009. https://sermons.logos.com/sermons/84052-are-you-god'-wife.

Macmillan, John A. 1932. *The Authority of the Believer.* Grapevine India. https://www.amazon.com/gp/product/B09ZV76Q9B/.

Missler, Chuck. September 1, 1996. "The Armor of God, Our Quest for Truth. *Koinonia House.* https://www.khouse.org/articles/1996/67/print/

Missler, Chuck. December 1, 1996. "The Shield of Faith: The Armor of God." *Koinonia House.* https://www.khouse.org/articles/1996/268/.

Renner, Rick. *Dressed to Kill: A Biblical Approach to Spiritual Warfare.* 2nd ed. Tulsa, OK: Harrison House Publishers, 2007, 2013.

Roat, A. June 22, 2020. "What is hermeneutics? History and methods of biblical interpretation." *Christianity Today.* https://www.christianity.com/wiki/bible/meaning-origin-history-of-biblical-hermeneutics.html

Siler, Josie. "What Is the Breastplate of Righteousness in the Armor of God?" *Christianity.Com.* September 22, 2022. https://www.christianity.com/wiki/christian-terms/what-is-the-breastplate-of-righteousness.html.

StudyLight.org. "Ephesians 6 - Barnes' Notes on the Whole Bible - Bible Commentaries." *StudyLight.org,* n.d. https://www.studylight.org/commentaries/eng/bnb/ephesians-6.html.

Bibliography

StudyLight.org. "Ephesians 6 - Dr. Constable's Expository Notes - Bible Commentaries." *StudyLight.org*, n.d. https://www.studylight.org/commentaries/eng/dcc/ephesians-6.html.

Tennant, Tracy. *Confessions of an Ex-Mormon: What I Wish I Knew When I Left the Church*. Olathe, KS, Right Track Publishing, 2017

Ulvog, Jim. "Balteus or cingulum- belt worn by Roman Legionnaires. Pugio – dagger carried by soldiers." *Ancient Finances*, July 6, 2019. https://ancientfinances.com/2019/07/06/balteus-or-cingulum-belt-worn-by-roman-legionnaires-puglio-dagger-carried-by-soldiers/.

Unknown, "A New Pair of Shoes." *Inspirational Stories*, February 3, 2020, https://www.inspirationalstories.com/new-pair-of-shoes-a/.

Walden, Jamie. "Supernatural Healing! ~ Finley's Testimony," September 13, 2023. https://www.youtube.com/watch?v=m95X8h-L8jM.

Wieja, Estera. "What Did Jesus Mean by Repent? The Hebrew Meaning of Teshuva." *FIRM Israel*, January 18, 2023. https://firmisrael.org/learn what-did-jesus-mean-by-repent-the-hebrew-meaning-of-teshuva/.

"World Watch List 2024," n.d. https://www.opendoors.org/en-US/persecution/countries/.

About the Author

Tracy Tennant is an author, engaging speaker, teacher, and mother of 10 children. As a homeschooling mom for over 16 years, she experienced countless adventures on family road trips that spanned states from the West to East coasts.

Tracy graduated *summa cum laude* with a degree in communication studies. Her area of ministry is in spiritual warfare training and inner healing and deliverance. Her passion is teaching biblical truth for the equipping of the saints.

Books

Mormonism, the Matrix, and Me:
My Journey from Kolob to Calvary
Details her spiritual journey out of Mormonism into biblical faith.

Confessions of an Ex-Mormon:
What I Wish I Knew When I Left the Church

Confessions of an Ex-Mormon Recovery Journal

No Excuses Reading Journal
Self-guided reading journals to keep track of the books you read and keep notes on them. For various book genres.

Visit Tracy's website: TheMormonMatrix.com

Listen to her podcast **From Kolob to Calvary**
Available on iTunes and other platforms.

To contact the author for speaking engagements, comments or questions , email:

TracyTennant@outlook.com

www.ingramcontent.com/pod-product-compliance
Lightning Source LLC
Chambersburg PA
CBHW070104080526
44586CB00013B/1184